STRATEGIC SPIRITUAL WARFARE

STRATEGIC SPIRITUAL WARFARE

ARMING YOURSELF FOR BATTLE, WINNING THE SPIRITUAL WAR

Ray Beeson and Patricia Hulsey

OM

Overcomers Ministries
Ventura, CA

Copyright © 1995, 2006 by Ray Beeson and Patricia Hulsey

Published by Overcomers Ministries, Ventura, CA   ISBN 0-9748269-1-X

All rights reserved. Written permission must be secured from the publisher to use or reproduce any part of this book, except for brief quotations in critical reviews, articles, or books.

Formerly Published by Thomas Nelson, Inc., Publishers with
ISBN 0-7852-7972-5.

Unless otherwise noted, Scripture quotations are from the NEW KING JAMES VERSION of the Bible. Copyright © 1979, 1980, 1982, 1990, Thomas Nelson, Inc., Publishers.

Scripture quotations noted KJV are from The Holy Bible, KING JAMES VERSION.

Scripture quotations noted NIV are taken from the HOLY BIBLE, NEW INTERNATIONAL VERSION®. Copyright © 1973, 1978, 1984 by International Bible Society.
The "NIV" and "New International Version" trademarks are registered in the United States Patent and Trademark Office by International Bible Society. Use of either trademark requires the permission of the International Bible Society.

Scripture quotations noted TLB are from *The Living Bible* (Wheaton, Illinois: Tyndale House Publishers, 1971).

Scripture quotations noted RSV are from the REVISED STANDARD VERSION of the Bible. Copyright © 1946, 1952, 1971, 1973 by the Division of the Christian Education of the National Council of the Churches of Christ in the USA.

Excerpts from *The Real Battle* by Ray Beeson, © 1988 by Tyndale House Publishers, are included in this work.

Printed in the United States of America

From Ray—

To Amy:

Your dad deeply loves, admires,

and respects you.

* * *

From Patricia—

This book is also lovingly dedicated

to three of God's mighty spiritual warriors:

- My father, ELLIS PAT MURPHY, whose prayers strengthen me in the midst of spiritual conflict,

- My good friend, DR. MORRIS CERULLO, who taught me how to war effectively against the enemy,

- My husband, ARGIS DANIEL HULSEY, my dearest comrade in the battles of life.

The noise of a multitude in the mountains,

Like that of many people!

A tumultuous noise of the kingdoms

of nations gathered together!

The LORD of hosts musters

The army for battle.

Isaiah 13:4

Contents

STRATEGIC SPIRITUAL WARFARE

Introduction xi

Part One—The Call to Arms: A Summons to the Invisible War

1. Open Your Spiritual Eyes 3

Part Two—Induction: Becoming Part of the Army of God

2. Join God's Army 21

Part Three—Basic Training: Preparing for War

3. Identify the Enemy 35
4. Survey Enemy Territory 57
5. Meet the Captain of God's Army 73
6. Complete Basic Training 83

Part Four—Mobilization: Active Military Service in God's Army

7. Arm Yourself with Defensive Weapons 103
8. Arm Yourself with Offensive Weapons 118
9. Employ Offensive and Defensive Strategies 128

Part Five—Invasion: Entering the Combat Zone

10. Take Strategic Territory 147
11. Resist Enemy Propaganda 179
12. Set the Captives Free 187
13. Rescue the Wounded 203
14. Deliver the Demonized 222

Part Six—The Final Briefing: The Last Great Battle of Spiritual Warfare

15. Prepare for the Final Conflict 251

Bibliography 261

Notes 267

About the Authors 271

Introduction
STRATEGIC SPIRITUAL WARFARE

If you were to select one word to describe your daily life, what would it be? Routine? Boring? Stressful? Pleasurable?

For many of us, *struggle* may come to mind. Often, life seems like a battle against discouragement, disappointment, and depression. We wrestle against a maze of difficult circumstances that may include a broken home, failing relationships, poor health, or diminishing finances. In the midst of such battles, we may feel we are all alone, that no other "mature" believers have such problems.

Let us dispel one lie of the enemy up front. You are not alone in your struggles. God's Word, the Bible, describes many men and women who faced difficult battles. In fact, the apostle Paul spoke of life as combat, conflict, and continual wrestling, not only in the natural realm, but in the spiritual realm as well.

No subject in Scripture is more controversial or difficult to discuss than spiritual warfare. Many people either have an aversion to talking about Satan and demons, or they tend to overemphasize the enemies of our soul.

We must remember that the Western mind-set is quite different from that of the cultures to which the Bible was originally delivered. In order to really understand the world in which we live and God's desire for it, we must accept instruction from the Holy Spirit toward a different mind-set that incorporates the spirit world. Jesus recognized the daily struggles we all face. He acknowledged a very real spiritual enemy, and He provided effective strategic spiritual guidelines for dealing with him.

INTRODUCTION

We need to understand these strategies and know how to put them into action. Through *Strategic Spiritual Warfare*, you will not only learn about spiritual warfare, but you will also begin to *do* warfare through a fifteen-step interactive program that will guide you in facing the natural and spiritual battles of life.

How to Use This Workbook

In each lesson you will find:

A Step to Take: Each chapter title reflects an action step.

Objectives: Each spiritual warfare strategy session contains specific goals.

Key Verses for This Study: Each session lists several Scripture verses for memorization to further your study.

Written in an interactive format, each of the fifteen lessons will ask you to respond and to apply your learning. We believe the Holy Spirit will help you understand and use spiritual warfare strategies more effectively as a result of studying this material.

God is building a great and mighty army. Listen closely with your spiritual ears and you will hear the summons to battle. In the process, however, please keep one principle always before you: Be God conscious, not demon conscious. Know your enemy and how to fight him, but keep your mind and attention focused on Jesus.

Fifteen Strategies to Win Spiritual Battles

1. Open Your Spiritual Eyes
2. Join God's Army
3. Identify the Enemy
4. Survey Enemy Territory
5. Meet the Captain of God's Army
6. Complete Basic Training
7. Arm Yourself with Defensive Weapons
8. Arm Yourself with Offensive Weapons
9. Employ Offensive and Defensive Strategies
10. Take Stragetic Territory
11. Resist Enemy Propaganda
12. Set the Captives Free
13. Rescue the Wounded
14. Deliver the Demonized
15. Prepare for the Final Conflict

Part One: The Call to Arms

A SUMMONS TO THE INVISIBLE WAR

A great war is being waged in the spiritual world: a personal battle between the flesh and the spirit, a social battle greatly influenced by the forces of evil, a spiritual battle against evil supernatural powers.

In Old Testament times a trumpet summoned God's people to fight. Today, a spiritual appeal sounds throughout the nations of the world. It summons us to the invisible war. God is calling His people to arms.

1 OPEN YOUR SPIRITUAL EYES

Objectives: Through this strategy session, you will learn to:

- Describe the natural and spiritual realms
- Identify the two spiritual kingdoms
- Discuss the real war
- Explain how the war started
- Relate the reason for this present war
- State the basic principle of spiritual warfare
- Identify the kingdom to which you belong

Key Verses for This Study:

> For we do not wrestle against flesh and blood, but against principalities, against powers, against the rulers of the darkness of this age, against spiritual hosts of wickedness in the heavenly places. (Eph. 6:12)

> The thief does not come except to steal, and to kill, and to destroy. I have come that they may have life, and that they may have it more abundantly. (John 10:10)

> He who sins is of the devil, for the devil has sinned from the beginning. For this purpose the Son of God was manifested, that He might destroy the works of the devil. (1 John 3:8)

And that they may come to their senses and escape the snare of the devil, having been taken captive by him to do his will. (2 Tim. 2:26)

Lest Satan should take advantage of us; for we are not ignorant of his devices. (2 Cor. 2:11)

Step One: Open Your Spiritual Eyes

Mankind has always believed in unseen creatures peopling the aerial spaces. The Bible sustains this idea, informing us that these spiritual intelligences do exist, and in close proximity to our world; that they are divided into two vast hosts: the one active in good ministries for our race; the other intent on annoying and injuring us; the one host designated as angels, loyal to God; the other called demons, apostates under Satan and rebels against God.

—Mrs. George Needham

To understand the invisible war, we must first understand the two worlds in which we live.

The apostle Paul said, "There is a natural body, and there is a spiritual body" (1 Cor. 15:44). We can see, feel, touch, hear, and taste the natural world. It is tangible and for the most part visible.

But there is also another world in which we live—the spiritual world. We cannot see it with our physical eyes, but it is real nevertheless.

We seldom recognize the spiritual realm because we are separated from God and therefore not as sensitive as we should be. Our spiritual blindness keeps us from seeing past our natural senses: "But the natural man does not receive the things of the Spirit of

God, for they are foolishness to him; nor can he know them, because they are spiritually discerned" (1 Cor. 2:14).

Describe your natural world. What tangible struggles do you face (personal relationships, financial problems, job or professional issues)?
___
___

Describe your spiritual world. Do you feel isolated and alone or upheld by God? Can you reconcile your personal difficulties with the concept of a loving God?
___
___

Elisha had the ability to see into the spiritual world. During battle, troops from Syria surrounded a small town called Dothan, where Elisha was staying. Read the story in 2 Kings 6:8–22 and answer the following questions.

Why did the king of Syria want to capture Elisha?
___
___

Which army had the most soldiers?
___

How did Elisha respond to the multitude of soldiers, horses, and chariots that surrounded Dothan?
___

How did his servant, Gehazi, respond?
___
___

What happened to the king's soldiers to make them Elisha's prisoners?

_____

_____

This skirmish around Dothan parallels the conditions of our day. Some, like Elisha, can see clearly into the realm of the spirit. They understand what is happening spiritually on this planet.

Others, like Elisha's servant, need a little help to see and understand the spiritual world. These people are open to the truths of God's Word and ready to learn.

But, as in Dothan, many are spiritually asleep and cannot see into this higher dimension. Content to live in the natural realm, they do not want to confront things beyond their senses. Out of a concern that too much attention might be given to understanding the unseen world, some give it no attention at all. Still others do not want their attraction to this present life threatened and busily continue to build earth's kingdoms, not even considering eternity.

Which attitude do you hold toward spiritual warfare?

____ The attitude of Elisha
____ The attitude of Gehazi
____ The attitude of the people of Dothan

Which do you desire to develop in the future?

____ The attitude of Elisha
____ The attitude of Gehazi
____ The attitude of the people of Dothan

Do you think your current battles have anything to do with the spiritual realm? Explain:

_____

_____

Do you believe in a personal spiritual enemy?

Two Spiritual Kingdoms

Within the natural and spiritual realms there exist natural and spiritual kingdoms. (*Kingdom* refers to rulership.) Like the natural realm, the spiritual realm has very real leaders.

The Bible says that the evil part of the spiritual kingdom rules the natural kingdoms of this world. The leader is a persona sometimes called Lucifer but is more often referred to as Satan or the devil:

> Then the devil, taking Him up on a high mountain, showed Him all the kingdoms of the world in a moment of time. And the devil said to Him, "All this authority I will give You, and their glory; *for this has been delivered to me, and I give it to whomever I wish.*" (Luke 4:5–6, italics added)

The kingdom of Satan consists of Satan, demons, and all people who live in sin and rebellion against God. Satan's control, however, is limited and will someday end. God has a plan to change things and bring all the kingdoms of the world under God's authority: "Then the seventh angel sounded: And there were loud voices in heaven, saying, *'The kingdoms of this world have become the kingdoms of our Lord and of His Christ*, and He shall reign forever and ever!'" (Rev. 11:15, italics added). This is "to be put into effect when the times will have reached their fulfillment—to bring all things in heaven and on earth together under one head, even Christ" (Eph. 1:10 NIV).

God's kingdom consists of God (Father, Son, and Holy Spirit), angels, and all people who live in loving submission to Him. Every person alive is a resident of one of these two kingdoms. We can enter the kingdom of God only through the agency and finished work of Jesus Christ. We must consciously and individually accept Christ as our agent. God the Father has designated Him to handle the legalities in making a change of kingdoms: "Nor is there salvation in any other, for there is no other name under heaven given among men by which we must be saved" (Acts 4:12).

Most people realize that we have been born into a decadent kingdom. In 1 John 5:19 we read that "the whole world is under the control of the evil one." We entered this wicked kingdom through birth. "Behold, I was brought forth in iniquity, / And in sin my mother conceived me" (Ps. 51:5).[1]

Identify the inhabitants of God's spiritual kingdom.
_____

Identify the spiritual forces of evil.
_____

How did we become part of the evil kingdom?
_____
_____

Who can help us change kingdoms?
_____

The Real War

Just as there are wars fought in the natural realm, there are also real battles in the spiritual realm. As natural warfare is understood with a natural mind, so spiritual warfare must be understood with a spiritual mind.

Many of us consider the spiritual battle as one of God against Satan. Contrary to the writings of Dante, Milton, and Goethe, the battle is not between God and Satan. God has no enemies that pose Him a threat, for He is stronger than anyone or anything. Rather, the battle rages between those who are rebelling against Him and those who want to serve Him.

We are not pawns in a giant cosmic chess game. God has given us the ability to choose, and in choosing we have rebelled against Him. The question now is whether we will be restored to God and learn to live in harmony with Him. Satan is a catalyst for our rebellion, and because we chose to disobey God, the enemy now holds significant power over us.

Our major battles in life are not against people. They are against demonic spirits: "For we do not wrestle against flesh and blood, but against principalities, against powers, against the rulers of the darkness of this age, against spiritual hosts of wickedness in the heavenly places" (Eph. 6:12). No one is removed from this battle. All of us are engaged in this struggle whether we like it or not and whether we acknowledge it or not. No one can view it from a distance; there is no neutral ground.

Read the first two chapters of Job and answer the following questions.

What kind of man was Job?
_____
_____

Summarize the problems he faced.
_____
_____

Was there some secret sin in Job's life that resulted in his trials?
_____
_____

Who initiated the conversation between God and Satan?

Why did God allow Satan to touch Job's life?

How did Job respond to his problems?

How did his wife respond?

What problems have you encountered in your life? How did you respond? Could you have responded more appropriately based on what you learned in Job 1-2?

When things go poorly in your life, do you become angry with or blame God?

Examine the real war that believers face. Where does it occur?

Who are the opponents?

The battle between the two kingdoms is really a battle between:

How the War Started

God created Lucifer, a beautiful angel, and exalted him to high prominence. His name means "brightness" or that which "shines." But Lucifer decided to try to take over God's kingdom. You may read about his rebellion in Isaiah 14:12-17 and in Ezekiel 28:12-19.

A group of angels joined Lucifer in this revolt. God's holy angels cast them out. Lucifer, now called Satan ("adversary, accuser, or slanderer" because of his character change), and the sinful angels formed their own kingdom on earth.

Jesus said He *saw* this event take place. "And He said to them, 'I saw Satan fall like lightning from heaven'" (Luke 10:18). Notice He did not say that He was involved. Keep in mind that the battle is not between God and Satan but rather between those who have submitted to God (angels and redeemed people) and those who have rebelled against God (fallen angels and unredeemed people).

> And you He made alive, who were dead in trespasses and sins, in which you once walked according to the course of this world, according to the prince of the power of the air, the spirit who now works in the sons of disobedience. (Eph. 2:1-2)

Satan and his angels *fell,* whereas people *die.* The Bible does not say that we are *fallen;* it says we are *dead.* The word *death* in Scripture connotes separation. Our sins have separated us from God.

After reading the biblical accounts of Satan's fall, answer the following questions.

List the five "I will" statements made by Lucifer in Isaiah 14:12-14.

I will _____
I will _____

STRATEGIC SPIRITUAL WARFARE

I will _____
I will _____
I will _____

Summarize the prophecy in Isaiah 14:15–17 concerning Lucifer.
_____
_____

According to Ezekiel 28:14–15, what previous position did Lucifer hold in heaven?
_____
_____

What do you think motivated Lucifer's sin (see Ezek. 28:17)?
_____
_____

Lucifer means: _____

Satan means: _____

What was Satan's basic sin? _____

Lucifer's fall resulted from an act of will. List any spiritual falls you have taken because of a willful act:
_____
_____

The Reason for This Present War

God originally created us in His image and for His glory (Gen. 2). Literally, God created us in order to provide a bride for His Son—a wife for the Lamb (Rev. 19, 21). Perhaps Satan rebelled out of pride and jealousy, because he felt that the creation of people would take something away from him. Whatever his reason, he is determined to destroy us. His ultimate plan is to separate us from God in order to do so.

In Genesis 3, we learn that our involvement in the invisible war started when Adam and Eve yielded to temptation in the Garden of Eden. Satan influenced the first man and his wife to disobey God, thus beginning sin within the human race. Adam and Eve joined Satan in his rebellion against God, resulting in our inheriting a nature opposed to God, a nature that constantly disobeys Him. "Therefore, just as through one man sin entered the world, and death through sin, and thus death spread to all men, because all sinned" (Rom. 5:12).

This mind-set, received at birth, has been programmed into us through the constant influence of demon spirits upon our forefathers. We sometimes call this the Adamic (after Adam) nature or old nature. But our tendencies toward sin or "sin nature" are different from the Adamic or "old nature." Sin nature is our yearning to please our bodies at the expense of our spirits while old nature has to do with rebellion against God. We will examine these topics in greater detail later.

Our sin not only separates us from God but also puts us under Satan's control. First John 5:19 says "the whole world is under the control of the evil one" (NIV). Although this is true, it is important to realize that God *owns* this planet. He *leased* it to Adam who in effect gave it to Satan when Adam disobeyed God.

In John 10:10 we read: "The thief does not come except to steal, and to kill, and to destroy. I have come that they may have life, and that they may have it more abundantly." Satan wants to destroy us while God strives to save us from our waywardness and evil deeds.

Because God refuses to force Himself upon anyone, Satan appears to be nearly as strong as God in his involvement with us. God waits patiently for us to come to Him in loving submission. As a result, there exists an invisible war between us and the forces of evil. Often we lose many battles to sin.

Through our sin, we become separated from God and condemned to death (eternal separation). We actually face two deaths: The first is the separation of the body from the soul and spirit; the second is separation from the presence of God for eternity. But God loved us so much that He made a special plan to save us:

> For God so loved the world that He gave His only begotten Son, that whoever believes in Him should not perish but have everlasting life. For God did not send His Son into the world to condemn the world, but that the world through Him might be saved. (John 3:16–17)

The death and resurrection of Jesus not only resulted in our salvation from sin, but also initiated the defeat of Satan and his demons: "He who sins is of the devil, for the devil has sinned from the beginning. For this purpose the Son of God was manifested, that He might destroy the works of the devil" (1 John 3:8).

Although Jesus *began* the process to defeat Satan, He passed the responsibility for finishing the work to His body, the Church, composed of all those who have accepted His salvation. By fighting and conquering under the authority of Jesus, the Church is gaining on-the-job training for eventual rulership of the entire universe.[2]

Who currently rules the earth (see John 12:31 and Matt. 4:8–11)?

_____

Who owns the earth (see Ps. 24:1)?

_____

What has caused this present spiritual war (see John 10:10)?

_____

_____

According to Genesis 3, disobedience to God caused two horrible things to happen. What were they?

_____

_____

According to 1 Corinthians 15, what has resulted from the death and resurrection of Jesus?

_____

_____

The Basic Principle of Warfare

To effectively fight in the spiritual war now being waged on this planet, we must first trust Christ to save us. We must then become aware of Satan's goals and motives and of the spiritual strategies for overcoming him and his demons. As we gradually attain this knowledge, we must also begin to apply it.

Satan's demons work diligently to keep us from knowing that they exist and how they function; keeping us ignorant is one of their major goals. But the apostle Paul said it is important to know the enemy's strategies "lest Satan should take advantage of us; for we are not ignorant of his devices" (2 Cor. 2:11).

We must recognize that the battles of life, whether spiritual, emotional, mental, financial, or relational are all outward manifestations of a direct or an indirect spiritual cause.

We are called to intelligent combat. Without becoming preoccupied with the subject, we must learn everything we can about spiritual warfare.

Although many things seem to result from the circumstances of life, the basis of these natural events is found in the spiritual world. We have tried to correct the evils around us through education, legislation, and hard physical work. The evils of this world, caused in the spiritual realm, cannot be corrected by natural means.

Examine each of the following areas of your life and identify battles that may face you:

Physical: _____

Spiritual: _____

Emotional: _____

Mental: _____

Financial: _____

Relational: _____

Think about each of these areas. What spiritual factors may be underlying your natural battles?
_____
_____

To Which Kingdom Do You Belong?

One of the parables Jesus told illustrates that all people are either part of Satan's kingdom or part of God's kingdom. Jesus compared the world to a field. In it, the good seed represented God's children. The bad seed, which grew into weeds, represented the children of the wicked one: "The field is the world, the good seeds are the sons of the kingdom, but the tares are the sons of the wicked one. The enemy who sowed them is the devil" (Matt. 13:38–39).

The Bible teaches that we are born in sin, that we have a basic nature, or "seed," of sin within us. Our natural inclination is to do wrong: "Therefore, just as through one man sin entered the world, and death through sin, and thus death spread to all men, because all sinned" (Rom. 5:12).

There are only two divisions in the invisible war. Jesus said, "He who is not with Me is against Me" (Luke 11:23). We cannot be neutral but must either choose one side or the other. We are either victors or victims. We are either part of God's army or a part of the enemy's kingdom.

To which kingdom do you belong?
____ The kingdom of God.   ____ The kingdom of Satan.

God's Word appeals to us to move from the evil kingdom of self and Satan to God's kingdom. Chapter 2 of this manual explains how to do this as you enlist in God's spiritual army.

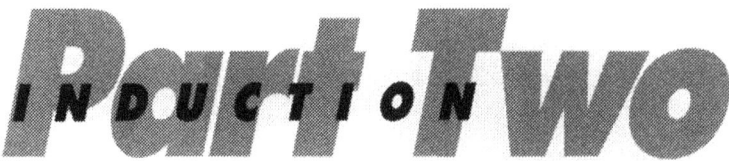

Part Two
INDUCTION

BECOMING PART OF
THE ARMY OF GOD

All armies in the natural world have induction procedures—steps you must take to join the forces. The spiritual army also has specific requirements for joining the troops. Are you ready to become part of God's army?

2 JOIN GOD'S ARMY

Objectives: Through this strategy session, you will learn to:

- Define *conversion*
- Explain the importance of conversion
- Explain why repentance is necessary for conversion
- Discuss the importance of repentance
- Explain what causes people to repent
- Define *confession*
- Compare the story of the prodigal son to prodigal man
- Define *justification*
- List the effects of salvation

Key Verses for This Study:

> For God so loved the world that He gave His only begotten Son, that whoever believes in Him should not perish but have everlasting life. (John 3:16)

> Nor is their salvation in any other, for there is no other name under heaven given among men by which we must be saved. (Acts 4:12)

> Jesus answered and said to him, "Most assuredly, I say to you, unless one is born again, he cannot see the kingdom of God." (John 3:3)

That if you confess with your mouth the Lord Jesus and believe in your heart that God has raised Him from the dead, you will be saved. For with the heart one believes unto righteousness, and with the mouth confession is made unto salvation. For the Scripture says, "Whoever believes on Him will not be put to shame." (Rom. 10:9–11)

Step Two: Join God's Army

So the chief thing He did was to call men. His presence was a call, and the crowds flocked to Him wherever He went. His life of purity and sympathy was felt as an earnest call and responded to eagerly. His doings were a very intense call. Every healed man and woman, every one set free of demon influence, every one of the fed multitudes, felt called to this man who had helped them so. His teaching was a continual call, and His preaching. But above all else stood out the personal call He gave men. For our Lord Jesus was not content to deal with the crowds simply; He dealt with men one by one in intimate heart touch.
—S. D. Gordon

In the previous chapter we discussed the two kingdoms, one of submission to God and the other of rebellion against Him. In this chapter we will discover in more detail God's wonderful plan that enables us to leave the evil kingdom and enter the righteous one. To enlist in God's army, you must change kingdoms. (If you have already joined God's army, this chapter can still serve as an important reminder of the elements of your salvation.)

The Meaning of Conversion

The word *conversion*, which means "to turn," is often used to refer to the changing of kingdoms. When used in connection with biblical repentance, conversion means to "turn from the wrong way to the right way." "And the hand of the Lord was with them, and a great number believed and turned to the Lord" (Acts 11:21).

Conversion is turning from the darkness of sin to the light of God's righteousness, "to open their eyes, in order to turn them from darkness to light" (Acts 26:18). It is turning from the power of Satan to the power of God.

Conversion also involves turning from worldly things to God and from false gods to the one true God. Conversion means being "born again" spiritually. "Jesus answered and said to him, 'Most assuredly, I say to you, unless one is born again, he cannot see the kingdom of God'" (John 3:3).

In your own words, write out the meaning of conversion.
_____

Have you been converted? ___ Yes ___ No

The Importance of Conversion

Conversion is a process that involves change. As Matthew 18:3 warns us, this change must happen for us to enter the kingdom of heaven. It saves us from spiritual death, the eternal separation from God.

> Assuredly, I say to you, unless you are converted and become as little children, you will by no means enter the kingdom of heaven.

Why is conversion important?
_____

Repentance and Conversion

Conversion and repentance are related. *Repentance* means "to change one's mind," to make a personal and voluntary decision to forsake sin and enter into fellowship with God.

But repentance that results in conversion cannot happen without God's help. That is why God sent His Son Jesus. Only Jesus is capable of providing the help we need to turn to God. Acts 4:12 tells us that salvation cannot occur through any other but Jesus: "Nor is there salvation in any other, for there is no other name under heaven given among men by which we must be saved."

What does repentance mean?
_____

How are conversion and repentance related?
_____

The Importance of Repentance

Repentance is considered a foundation for the Christian faith for the following reasons:

- God commands it: "In the past God overlooked such ignorance, but now he commands all people everywhere to repent" (Acts 17:30 NIV).
- It is necessary to avoid spiritual death: ". . . but unless you repent you will all likewise perish" (Luke 13:3).
- It is necessary to enter God's kingdom: "From that time Jesus began to preach and to say, 'Repent, for the kingdom of heaven is at hand'" (Matt. 4:17).

- God desires it for all: "The Lord is not slack concerning His promise, as some count slackness, but is longsuffering toward us, not willing that any should perish but that all should come to repentance" (2 Peter 3:9).
- It is the reason Jesus came into the world: "I have not come to call the righteous, but sinners, to repentance" (Luke 5:32).
- It is the message that Jesus preached: "Now after John was put in prison, Jesus came to Galilee preaching the gospel of the kingdom of God and saying, 'The time is fulfilled, and the kingdom of God is at hand. Repent, and believe in the gospel'" (Mark 1:14–15).
- It is the message the disciples preached: "So they went out and preached that people should repent" (Mark 6:12).
- It is the message we are still to preach today: "Then He said to them, 'Thus it is written, and thus it was necessary for the Christ to suffer and to rise from the dead the third day, and that repentance and remission of sins should be preached in His name to all nations'" (Luke 24:46–47).

Summarize the importance of repentance.

If you have not enlisted in God's army through confession and repentance, you have a wonderful opportunity to do so right now! According to 2 Corinthians 6:2, today is the day for your salvation. You can receive this wonderful gift from God by praying this prayer:

> Dear Heavenly Father,
>
> I come to you in the name of your Son, Jesus Christ. I acknowledge my sins before you. I repent of my sins. I accept Jesus Christ as my Savior and the Lord of my life. Thank you for your provision of salvation for me. In Jesus' name, Amen.

What Causes Us to Repent?

Since repentance is a foundation on which the Christian faith rests, and as believers we have a responsibility for spreading its message throughout the world, we must understand how others will be persuaded to repent from sin.

Jesus said no one could come to Him unless God the Father enabled that person to do so. God draws us to repentance (John 6:44). As Romans 2:4 reveals, the goodness of God leads people to repent: "Or do you despise the riches of His goodness, forbearance, and longsuffering, not knowing that the goodness of God leads you to repentance?"

The preaching of the Word of God also causes people to repent:

> Then Peter said to them, "Repent, and let every one of you be baptized in the name of Jesus Christ for the remission of sins." . . . Then those who gladly received his word were baptized; and that day about three thousand souls were added to them. (Acts 2:38, 41)

What causes people to repent?
_____
_____
_____

What caused you to repent?

    ___ The goodness of God
    ___ Preaching and teaching
    ___ The example of a Christian friend
    ___ Other: _____

List the names of friends or relatives for whose salvation you pray. What practical actions might you take to draw them to accept Jesus Christ as their Savior?

Confession

The word *confess* comes from the Greek *homologeo*, which means "to assent or acknowledge."

To accomplish our goal of conversion, we must turn around and go in another direction—that is, we must repent. In order to do this, we must acknowledge our sin. Once we are convinced, by God's help, of our depraved condition, we move toward victory by first confessing the wrong we have discovered. "If we confess our sins, He is faithful and just to forgive us our sins and to cleanse us from all unrighteousness" (1 John 1:9).

Summarize the meaning of *confession*.

The Prodigal Son and Us

Jesus illustrated conversion and repentance through a story about a rebellious son. (Read Luke 15:11-24.) This young man left his father and his home, went to a distant land, and wasted all he owned. Hungry, lonely, in rags, and tending pigs, he finally realized his lowly condition and felt sorry for his actions.

Then he made an important decision. He said, "I will set out and go back to my father." This inward decision resulted in a change of outward action; he changed the direction of his life and went home to seek forgiveness.

Notice the process the son went through in verses 17 and 19. He repented. He "changed his mind." The young man realized his sinful condition and decided to go to his father and confess his sin. Conversion came about when he acted on his decision. Verse 20 records how the young man left his old life and started a new one.

We need to make similar decisions. We must come to our senses like the prodigal and recognize our spiritual condition. We must make a decision that will result in a change of spiritual direction, a change that will turn us from sin toward God.

"Behold, now is the accepted time; behold, now is the day of salvation" (2 Cor. 6:2). With this wonderful promise of the availability of salvation, why would we want to put this decision off for even a single day?

Explain how the story of the prodigal son illustrates conversion and repentance.

_____

_____

We are like the prodigal son. In our sinful condition we have our backs turned to God. Each day takes us farther away from God and closer to eternal separation. Looking back over your life, what specific steps have you taken away from God?

_____

_____

The story of the prodigal son is as much about the waiting father as about the wayward child. The story illustrates the father's tremendous love and forgiveness, acceptance and rejoicing. After patiently waiting for his son to return, the father throws a party in his honor.

Describe your return from sin to God.

_____
_____

Justification

Justification, a judicial term, means "to be free from blame or guilt." Repentance and confession that lead to conversion actually bring us to a place where our sins are not held against us—we will not have to pay for them. Although the penalty for sin is very great, God has offered a way for us to come to Him that frees us from any eternal consequences for our transgressions. We are justified, or declared free and blameless, through Jesus Christ, who paid the price for our sins on the cross. He took upon Himself our penalty so that we will "have peace with God" (Rom. 5:1), and we "shall be saved from wrath through Him" (Rom. 5:9). "For the Scripture says, 'Whoever believes on Him will not be put to shame'" (Rom. 10:11).

When justified by repenting and accepting Jesus Christ as Savior, we are saved not only from the penalties for sin but also from a life of sin. "Most assuredly, I say to you, he who hears My word and believes in Him who sent Me has everlasting life, and shall not come into judgment, but has passed from death into life" (John 5:24).

It is God's desire that we all obtain salvation rather than experience the wrath of God's judgment on sin.

> For God did not appoint us to wrath, but to obtain salvation through our Lord Jesus Christ. (1 Thess. 5:9)

> For God so loved the world that He gave His only begotten Son, that whoever believes in Him should not perish but have everlasting life. For God did not send His Son into the world

to condemn the world, but that the world through Him might be saved. (John 3:16–17)

Summarize the meaning of *justification*.
_____
_____

Do you feel guilty for things you have done in your life?
_____

Remember that if you are born again, you are freed of blame or guilt in these matters. Lift each issue to God in prayer and release your feelings of blame and guilt to Him.

From what penalties for sin has justification freed you?
_____

The Effects of Salvation

What actually takes place in the salvation experience? The apostle Paul wrote of the mystery of the Spirit of Christ taking up residence in the human spirit upon invitation. "To them God willed to make known what are the riches of the glory of this mystery among the Gentiles: which is *Christ in you,* the hope of glory" (Col. 1:27, italics added).

Christ *will* enter a human heart. "Behold, I stand at the door and knock. If anyone hears My voice and opens the door, I will come in to him and dine with him, and he with Me" (Rev. 3:20).

He enters our hearts and dwells within us through the Holy Spirit. Before Jesus left the earth, He told us He would pray that the Father would send us a helper, the Holy Spirit. The world would not receive Him, but Christ's followers would "for He dwells with you *and will be in you*" (John 14:17, italics added).

A changed life gives evidence of Christ living in an individual. "Therefore, if anyone is in Christ, he is a new creation; old things have passed away; behold all things have become new" (2 Cor. 5:17). We also see Christ in a person who keeps God's commandments (1 John 3:24).

What is the most significant change that has occurred in your life since you accepted Jesus as your personal Savior?
_____
_____

List some other changes in your life since then.
_____
_____

What changes do you see that still need to take place in your life?
_____
_____

When we are born again, we take the first major step toward waging effective warfare with the enemy. By transferring from the kingdom of Satan to the kingdom of God, we enlist in a great spiritual army. We join warriors from many nations that have waged this battle through the centuries and become part of God's troops, an army prepared for war.

Part Three
BASIC TRAINING

PREPARING FOR WAR

In the natural world, no soldier goes into battle without receiving basic training prior to entering the combat zone.

In this section you will learn to identify the enemy, survey enemy territory, and recognize the Captain of God's army. In basic training, you will receive the strategies necessary to mobilize your spiritual resources for effective battle.

3 IDENTIFY THE ENEMY

Objectives: Through this strategy session, you will learn to:

- Discuss Satan's origin, former position, fall, objectives, involvement with humanity, and sphere of activity
- Explain the basis of the real battle
- Identify the attributes of Satan
- List the names of Satan
- Distinguish between what Satan is and is not
- Identify demons as Satan's coworkers
- Identify activities of demons in general
- Recognize satanic attacks against Christians

Key Verses for This Study:

And the Lord said, "Simon, Simon! Indeed, Satan has asked for you, that he may sift you as wheat." (Luke 22:31)

Be sober, be vigilant; because your adversary the devil walks about like a roaring lion, seeking whom he may devour. Resist him, steadfast in the faith. (1 Peter 5:8-9)

Therefore submit to God. Resist the devil and he will flee from you. (James 4:7)

For we do not wrestle against flesh and blood, but against principalities, against powers, against the rulers of the darkness of this age, against spiritual hosts of wickedness in the heavenly places. (Eph. 6:12)

Step Three: Identify the Enemy

The modern western Christian has a difficult time processing much of the material found in the Bible, even the New Testament. We find there is a world where angels visit, demons manifest, dreams and visions guide, God intervenes, and signs and wonders occur. Has science, psychology and medicine replaced the need for Jesus' ministry of revelation and power? As westerners, we are often converted in Christianity as "Christian atheists." We believe in God the Father and in Jesus, but we do not believe in the spirit world.

This state of affairs has resulted in our inability to grasp and function in the realm of spirits, holy or otherwise. Third world converts who are not controlled by modern western theology/world view do not seem to suffer from this spiritual dysfunction. Western Christians often seem to be open intellectually while closed experientially. This need to think right while refusing to do right is counterproductive. We develop ingenious distancing tools to avoid dealing with the spiritual realm in general, and with demons in particular.

—*Steve Robbins*

In Chapter 1 we learned of the great invisible war in the spiritual realm. Now we will find out more about the chief characters in this conflict. We will focus primarily on the principal leader of the enemy—Satan—studying his goals and motives in order to counter his moves.

In the natural world, soldiers must identify the enemy before entering the battlefield. To plan strategy to win the conflict, soldiers must study all available information on their opponent. We must do the same.

Identifying our enemy in the spiritual war can be difficult because the forces of evil are not clothed in flesh. For this reason, we rely on the Word of God to help us understand the enemy's nature and strategies.

In the study of spiritual warfare, we must identify only those things directly attributable to Satan and demons. We must use caution in attributing events to their work if we have no actual evidence of their involvement. We can do more damage than good by "shadow boxing" the enemy.

Avoid a "demon-this" or a "demon-that" mentality. If we conclude that all problems in life result from satanic activity, we fail to recognize that humans carry a great deal of responsibility for earth's problems. Nowhere does Scripture call Satan and his demons responsible for all the evil that plagues us. If they were, God would not hold us accountable for our sin.

As you begin this study on the enemy, pray and ask God specifically for:

- A biblical understanding of the demonic realm
- Discernment for identifying that which is the direct result of demonic activity
- The ability to communicate what you learn to other Christians in a mature and nonthreatening manner
- The protection of the Holy Spirit for you and your family as you learn the truth

The Origin of Satan

Satan is a created being.[1] He did not exist until God created him through Jesus Christ, the second person of the Godhead.

All things were made through Him, and without Him nothing was made that was made. (John 1:3)

For by Him [Jesus Christ] all things were created that are in heaven and that are on earth, visible and invisible, whether thrones or dominions or principalities or powers. All things were created through Him and for Him. (Col. 1:16)

God created Satan (Lucifer), his highly honored angel, perfect—without sin. Like us, he had a free will and the ability to make decisions, thus giving him unique personality. But his ability to choose led him to make evil choices. "You were perfect in your ways from the day you were created, / Till iniquity was found in you" (Ezek. 28:15).

On the basis of Colossians 1:16 and Ezekiel 28:15, are the following statements true or false?

___ Jesus created Satan.
___ Satan was perfect when he was created.
___ Satan did not have a free will.

The Former Position of Satan

Read the biblical description of Satan in Ezekiel 28:12–17. The passage begins with what appears to be God's judgment of a man. A closer examination, however, reveals that it is also judgment of Satan, apparently influencing an earthly ruler.

Ezekiel painted a beautiful picture of Satan's splendor and power as God created him. He described Satan as a gem among precious stones. But a gem has no light of its own. Its beauty is in its ability to reflect light.

When God created Satan (Lucifer), He made him with a capacity to reflect God's glory, perhaps to a greater degree than any other created being. God's light made Lucifer radiate beauty.

Satan was originally an angel of the cherubim class.[2] In fact, he was a leader, perhaps a "guardian" or "covering" cherub.

Summarize what you have learned about Satan from Ezekiel 28:12–17.

_____

The Fall of Satan

Because of pride, Satan failed to retain his glorious position. The Bible describes his revolt and fall in Isaiah 14:12 and Ezekiel 28:17.

> How you are fallen from heaven,
> O Lucifer, son of the morning!
> How you are cut down to the ground,
> You who weakened the nations! (Isa. 14:12)

> Your heart was lifted up because of your beauty;
> You corrupted your wisdom for the sake
>   of your splendor;
> I cast you to the ground,
> I laid you before kings,
> That they might gaze at you. (Ezek. 28:17)

Why did Satan fall into sin?

_____

In Satan's rebellion, he originally sought to accomplish five goals as recorded in Isaiah 14:13–14.

I will ascend into heaven. He desired to occupy God's abode. God had perhaps given Satan a place of rulership outside of heaven, but Satan wanted heaven itself.

I will exalt my throne above the stars of God. Satan not only wanted the abode of God, but he also wanted to rule over the angelic host.

I will also sit on the mount of the congregation on the farthest sides of the north. The mount of the congregation seems to be where formal worship and praise to God takes place. Satan wanted to be glorified in God's place.

I will ascend above the heights of the clouds. Clouds speak of glory. (See Ex. 13:21; 40:28–34; Job 37:15–16; Matt. 26:64; Rev. 14:14–16, which show clouds in relationship to God's glory.) Satan apparently wanted God's glory for himself.

I will be like the Most High. Satan did not say that he would be God himself but that he would be *like* Him. Satan was after rulership and position that did not rightly belong to him.

Summarize Satan's original objectives.
_____
_____

Do you believe these are still Satan's objectives today? Why or why not?
_____
_____

God cast Satan out of heaven because of his sin. According to Revelation 12:7, angels actually carried out the task. "Therefore I cast you as a profane thing / Out of the mountain of God; / And I destroyed you, O covering cherub, / From the midst of the fiery stones. . . . I cast you to the ground" (Ezek. 28:16–17).

Satan's Involvement with Humanity

The Bible does not tell us specifically why Satan rebelled. Regardless of the reason for his fall, Satan hates and wants to destroy us. Both Scripture and history provide evidence that Satan's hatred is real. "The thief [Satan] does not come except to steal, and to kill, and to destroy" (John 10:10).

How Satan came to exist on earth with humans is a mystery. During Adam's initial reign, Satan had no authority on earth. God gave the planet to Adam, and he controlled it until he disobeyed God. We might better say that God leased or loaned earth to Adam, for the earth is the Lord's (Ps. 50:12; 89:11). Upon Adam's disobedience, the rulership of the world moved into Satan's hands. Jesus did not deny this rulership when Satan said to Him, "All this authority I will give You, and their glory; *for this has been delivered to me and, I give it to whomever I wish*" (Luke 4:6, italics added).

The mission of Jesus Christ was, and still is, to legally remove the rulership of earth from Satan's hands.

Satan's Sphere of Activity

Satan operates from earth, although he appears to have some access to heaven.

> Now there was a day when the sons of God came to present themselves before the LORD, and Satan also came among them. And the LORD said to Satan, "From where do you come?" So Satan answered the LORD and said, "From going to and fro on the earth, and from walking back and forth on it." (Job 1:6-7)

On earth he is known as the ruler of the air, possibly because air and spirit are often associated (see Eph. 2:2). Satan may work in direct relationship with the air itself, moving it to produce sounds that affect our subconscious like the subliminal messages we have learned to send each other.

Specifically, how has Satan worked against you?

_____

_____

The Basis of the Real Battle

Many nonChristians as well as many Christians follow a theology called *dualism*, the belief that Satan and God are arch enemies locked in combat. Dualism gives the impression that Satan can threaten God and that two great forces within the universe (good and evil) struggle against each other. However, the Bible gives us a different view.

First, the battle is not between God and Satan but between those who have submitted themselves to God and those who have rebelled against Him, both angels and humans. No one is even remotely capable of challenging or resisting God.

Second, the battle is not between good and evil. Jesus said that the only good person was God in heaven. The real battle, then, is between walking in the Spirit and walking in the flesh. (See Chapter 4 for an explanation of flesh.)

Third, the battle is not between success and failure. To a large degree, these terms express nonbiblical, cultural ideas. The battle is between obedience and disobedience to God.

Fourth, the battle is not between love and hate, but between love and lethargy. Love is an action, whereas hate is largely an attitude. Love and hate should not be compared, but love (an action) and lethargy (an inaction) are opposites.

Summarize what the battles of spiritual warfare concern.

_____

_____

The Attributes of Satan

Although Satan is a spirit, he is a real being with a personality and attributes. The Bible teaches that he is:

- Intelligent and subtle: "But I fear, lest somehow, as the serpent deceived Eve by his craftiness, so your minds may be corrupted from the simplicity that is in Christ" (2 Cor. 11:3).
- Emotional: "And the dragon was enraged with the woman, and he went to make war with the rest of her offspring, who keep the commandments of God and have the testimony of Jesus Christ" (Rev. 12:17).
- Self-willed: ". . . and that they may come to their senses and escape the snare of the devil, having been taken captive by him to do his will" (2 Tim. 2:26).
- Proud: ". . . lest being puffed up with pride he fall into the same condemnation as the devil" (1 Tim. 3:6).
- Powerful: "We know that we are of God, and the whole world lies under the sway of the wicked one" (1 John 5:19).

- Deceitful: "Put on the whole armor of God, that you may be able to stand against the wiles of the devil" (Eph. 6:11).
- Fierce and cruel: "Be sober, be vigilant; because your adversary the devil walks about like a roaring lion, seeking whom he may devour. Resist him, steadfast in the faith" (1 Peter 5:8–9).
- Deceptive: "And no wonder! For Satan himself transforms himself into an angel of light" (2 Cor. 11:14).

Summarize the attributes of Satan revealed in these verses.

_____

_____

The Names of Satan

The names of Satan reveal much about his personality. Besides Lucifer, which appears to be his given name, the Bible refers to him as follows:

Abaddon (Hebrew for "destroying angel"): Revelation 9:11
Accuser of our brethren: Revelation 12:10
Adversary: 1 Peter 5:8
Angel of the Abyss: Revelation 9:11 (NIV)
Angel of light: 2 Corinthians 11:14
Apollyon (Greek for "destroyer"): Revelation 9:11
Beelzebub: Matthew 12:24; Mark 3:22; Luke 11:15
Belial: 2 Corinthians 6:15
Deceiver: Revelation 12:9; 20:3
Destroyer: 1 Corinthians 10:10
Devil ("slanderer"): 1 Peter 5:8; Matthew 4:1
Dragon: Revelation 12:3, 9
Enemy: Matthew 13:39
Evil One: 1 John 5:19 (NIV)

IDENTIFY THE ENEMY

God of this age: 2 Corinthians 4:4
King of Tyre: Ezekiel 28:12–15
Liar, father of lies: John 8:44
Murderer: John 8:44
Prince of the demons: Matthew 12:24 (NIV)
Prince of this world: John 12:31; 14:30; 16:11 (NIV)
Roaring lion: 1 Peter 5:8
Ruler of darkness: Ephesians 6:12
Ruler of the kingdom of the air (prince of the power of the air): Ephesians 2:2 (NIV)
Ruler of this world: John 12:31; 14:30; 16:11
Satan ("adversary" or "opposer"): John 13:27
Serpent: Genesis 3:4, 14; Revelation 12:9
Tempter: Matthew 4:3; 1 Thessalonians 3:5

Review each name of Satan. Check those manifestations of Satan that you have experienced in your life. What happened? How did you respond? Were you successful? How could you have improved your response?

I Have Experienced	**What Happened**	**How I Responded**
___ Abaddon ("destroying angel")		
___ Accuser of our brethren		
___ Adversary		
___ Angel of the Abyss		
___ Angel of light		
___ Apollyon ("destroyer")		
___ Beelzebub		
___ Belial		
___ Deceiver		
___ Destroyer		
___ Devil ("slanderer")		

I Have Experienced	What Happened	How I Responded
___ Dragon	_____	_____
___ Enemy	_____	_____
___ Evil One	_____	_____
___ God of this age	_____	_____
___ King of Tyre	_____	_____
___ Liar, father of lies	_____	_____
___ Murderer	_____	_____
___ Prince of the demons	_____	_____
___ Prince of this world	_____	_____
___ Roaring lion	_____	_____
___ Ruler of darkness	_____	_____
___ Ruler of the kingdom of the air	_____	_____
___ Satan ("adversary" or "opposer")	_____	_____
___ Serpent	_____	_____
___ Tempter	_____	_____

In light of the nature of the enemy, the Bible gives two strong admonitions: "Be sober, be vigilant" (1 Peter 5:8) and ". . . do not . . . give place to the devil" (Eph. 4:26–27).

What Satan Is and Is Not

Satan is not omniscient (knowledgeable of all things). He has tremendous knowledge, but he does not know everything as God does.

Satan is not omnipotent (all powerful). The power of God within us is greater than the power of Satan. "You are of God, little children, and have overcome them, because He who is in you is greater than he who is in the world" (1 John 4:4).

Satan is strong only to those whom he is master. His power is limited by the power of God (see Job 1:10–12).

Satan is not omnipresent (present everywhere at the same time). He occupies only one place at one time. Satan does, however, have a great host of demon spirits that he dispatches throughout the earth to do his will and accomplish his purposes.

Review: Which of the following statements are true and which are false?

   ___ God is omnipotent.
   ___ Satan is omnipotent.
   ___ God is omnipresent.
   ___ Satan is omnipresent.
   ___ God is omniscient.
   ___ Satan is omniscient.

Demons—Satan's Coworkers

God created the angels. "For by Him all things were created that are in heaven and that are on earth, visible and invisible, whether thrones or dominions or principalities or powers. All things were created through Him and for Him" (Col. 1:16). When Lucifer rebelled against God, the angels who participated with him became known as demons[3] and were cast out of heaven:

> And war broke out in heaven: Michael and his angels fought against the dragon; and the dragon and his angels fought, but they did not prevail, nor was a place found for them in heaven any longer. So the great dragon was cast out, that serpent of

old, called the Devil and Satan, who deceives the whole world; he was cast to the earth, and his angels were cast out with him. (Rev. 12:7–9)

Second Peter 2:4 and Jude 6 reveal two groups of fallen angels. One group actively opposes God and His people on earth. The other group is confined in chains of darkness until the day of judgment. Satan, also called the "prince of demons" (Matt. 12:24 NIV), leads the host of active demons.

Throughout the Bible, demons serve Satan by doing his will and accomplishing his purposes. Their allegiance, however, is self-serving. They constitute the "power of the air" (Eph. 2:2) and the "power of darkness" (Col. 1:13).

The Attributes of Demons

Before being cast out of heaven, demons had the same attributes as the good angels. Note some of their attributes:

- Are spirits: Matthew 8:16; Luke 10:17, 20
- Can speak: Matthew 8:31; Mark 5:9, 12; Luke 8:28
- Believe: James 2:19
- Exercise their wills: Luke 8:32; 11:24
- Demonstrate intelligence: Mark 1:24
- Have emotions: Luke 8:28; James 2:19
- Recognize Jesus: Acts 19:15
- Have supernatural strength: Acts 19:16; Mark 5:3
- Have supernatural presence: Daniel 9:21–23
- Are eternal: Matthew 25:41
- Have their own doctrine: 1 Timothy 4:1–3
- Are evil: Matthew 10:1; Mark 1:27; 3:11

Have you witnessed demonic activity? Explain.
_____
_____

Have you observed situations where, although you were not certain, demonic activity appeared to be present? Explain.
_____
_____

Think about some of the problems you face today. Could demons be involved in any of them? Which difficulties have resulted from your own wrong choices?
_____
_____

The Names of Demons in Scripture

The New Testament refers to demons six times as evil spirits and twenty-three times as unclean spirits. They are called the devil's angels in Matthew 25:41.

The Organization of Demon Forces

Satan seeks to copy God, to do things as God does them. Satan is an imitator, not an originator. He has arrayed himself against us as a deceiver and a counterfeiter.

Satan's demons are organized in ranks similar to the organization of God's angelic host, as described in Colossians 1:16: "For by Him all things were created that are in heaven and that are on earth, visible and invisible, *whether thrones or dominions or principalities or powers.* All things were created through Him and for Him" (italics added).

Notice the demonic hierarchy: "For we do not wrestle against flesh and blood, *but against principalities, against powers, against the rulers of the darkness of this age, against spiritual hosts of wickedness in the heavenly places"* (Eph. 6:12, italics added).

Paul appears to have ranked the demons.[4] The following descriptions are what we believe may be the activities of each group:

1. *Principalities:* These demons are territorial. They live in one geographical area and do not seem to travel very far. Mountain ranges, rivers, lakes, and other natural divisions of land form their boundaries. When people move from one city to another, principalities do not usually follow.

2. *Powers:* Stronger than principalities, these demons are more mobile. "Powers" may actually inhabit people, whereas lesser demons are commissioned to harass and to wear people down to make them vulnerable to habitation. Lesser demons only enter a person after more powerful ones gain access.

3. *Rulers of the darkness:* These demons affect the overall spiritual condition of a place, for example, when the prince of the powers over Persia hindered the prayers of Daniel. This suggests that a single demon, or "strongman," is responsible for such activity.

4. *Spiritual hosts of wickedness in high places:* These appear to be the strongest of the demons, responsible for the development of spiritual counterfeits that keep people in bondage. These may be the demons who help to create belief systems such as Hinduism, Buddhism, Mormonism, and Satanism, and operate in major government centers.

Concerning these original followers of Satan, the Bible teaches the following:

Demons are somewhat united: Demons sometimes unite to possess a person. Luke 8:30 records the case of a man possessed by a legion of demons. And Mary Magdalene had seven demons (Luke 16:9).

Jesus spoke of the unity of demon powers, "If Satan casts out Satan, he is divided against himself. How then will his kingdom stand?" (Matt. 12:26).

Demons manifest different degrees of wickedness: This characteristic is illustrated by the demon who, when cast out, declared he would return with other evil spirits.

> When an unclean spirit goes out of a man, he goes through dry places, seeking rest, and finds none. Then he says, "I will return to my house from which I came." And when he comes, he finds it empty, swept, and put in order. Then he goes and takes with him seven other spirits more wicked than himself, and they enter and dwell there; and the last state of that man is worse than the first. So shall it also be with this wicked generation. (Matt. 12:43–45)

People delivered from demons do not have to allow them to return. They must first fill their house with the Holy Spirit so that it is occupied when the demons reappear, and then they must resist all the works of the enemy. "Therefore submit to God. Resist the devil and he will flee from you" (James 4:7).

Demons can change their function: The demon in 1 Kings 22:21–23 declared he would be a lying spirit. His statement "I will be" perhaps indicates that he was not previously a liar.

Demons serve different functions:

1. Evil spirits, responsible for influencing immoral acts and other kinds of evil, afflict the soul of humans. "And that very hour He cured many of infirmities, afflictions, and evil spirits; and to many blind He gave sight" (Luke 7:21).

2. Unclean spirits, if they serve in a different function from evil spirits, perhaps induce unclean thoughts in a person's mind. "And the unclean spirits, whenever they saw Him, fell down

before Him and cried out saying, 'You are the Son of God'" (Mark 3:11).

3. Spirits of infirmity afflict the body. "And behold, there was a woman who had a spirit of infirmity eighteen years, and was bent over and could in no way raise herself up" (Luke 13:11).

4. Deceiving spirits afflict the spirit, seducing people to believe lies and be damned to eternal punishment. These spirits produce false doctrines, cults, false Christs, and false teachers. "Now the Spirit expressly says that in latter times some will depart from the faith, giving heed to deceiving spirits and doctrines of demons" (1 Tim. 4:1).

How Demons Affect People

1. People can *have* an evil spirit (Matt. 11:18; Mark 7:25; Luke 4:33).
2. People can be *with* (Greek *in*) an evil spirit (Mark 5:2).
3. People can be *demonized* by (vexed with, influenced by, attacked with, possessed with) evil spirits (Matt. 4:24; Mark 1:32; Luke 8:36).

Do you recognize the influence of demon spirits in your life? If so, how is it manifested? How do you deal with demons? How might you improve your response?

Demonic Forces	How They Manifest	How I Deal with Them
___ Evil spirits		
___ Unclean spirits		
___ Spirits of infirmity		
___ Deceiving spirits		

Some Activities of Demons in General

Demons tempt: "Then Jesus, being filled with the Holy Spirit, returned from the Jordan and was led by the Spirit into the wilderness, being tempted for forty days by the devil" (Luke 4:1–2).

Demons deceive: "So the great dragon was cast out, that serpent of old, called the Devil and Satan, who deceives the whole world; he was cast to the earth, and his angels were cast out with him" (Rev. 12:9).

Demons oppress: ". . . Jesus of Nazareth . . . went about doing good and healing all who were oppressed by the devil" (Acts 10:38).

Demons bring the bondage of fear: "Inasmuch then as the children have partaken of flesh and blood, He Himself likewise shared in the same, that through death He might destroy him who had the power of death, that is, the devil, and release those who through fear of death were all their lifetime subject to bondage" (Heb. 2:14–15).

> For you did not receive the spirit of bondage again to fear, but you received the Spirit of adoption by whom we cry out, "Abba, Father." (Rom. 8:15)

Summarize what you have learned about demons.

List their names:
_____
_____

How are they organized?
_____
_____
_____

List their attributes:

_____
_____
_____

List their activities:

_____
_____
_____

Satanic Attacks Against Christians

Demons launch attacks in various ways in carrying out Satan's plans. They:

- Quote Scripture: Matthew 4:6
- Teach their own doctrines: 1 Timothy 4:1
- Transform themselves into angels of light: 2 Corinthians 11:14
- Encourage evil men to pervert righteousness: Acts 13:10
- Afflict the body: 2 Corinthians 12:7
- Tempt with hypocrisy and lying: Acts 5:3
- Sow tares (wicked people planted by the enemy in the midst of God's kingdom): Matthew 13:38-39
- Tempt with pride: 1 Timothy 3:6
- Produce counterfeit miracles, signs, and wonders: 2 Thessalonians 2:9
- Attempt to fill hearts with apostasy: John 13:27

Check those attacks of demons which you have experienced in your life. What happened? How did you deal with each attack? Were you successful? How could you have improved your response?

I Have Experienced Demons	What Happened	How I Responded
___ Quoting Scripture	_____	_____
___ Teaching their own doctrines	_____	_____
___ Transforming themselves into angels of light	_____	_____
___ Encouraging evil men to pervert righteousness	_____	_____
___ Afflicting the body	_____	_____
___ Tempting with hypocrisy and lying	_____	_____
___ Sowing tares	_____	_____
___ Tempting with pride	_____	_____
___ Producing counterfeit miracles, signs, and wonders	_____	_____
___ Attempting to fill the heart with apostasy	_____	_____

Some Accounts of Demons as Found in Scripture

To further your understanding of demonic powers, study the following scriptural accounts of demons. Check each passage as you read it:

Matthew
___ 4:1–11
___ 4:24
___ 8:16–17
___ 8:28–34
___ 9:32–34
___ 10:1, 8
___ 11:18
___ 12:22–30
___ 12:43–45
___ 13:19
___ 13:36–42
___ 15:22–28
___ 16:23
___ 17:14–21

Luke
___ 22:31

Acts
___ 13:10
___ 16:16–24
___ 26:18

2 Corinthians
___ 2:11
___ 11:13
___ 12:7–10
Ephesians
___ 6:11–12
Colossians
___ 2:15
1 Thessalonians
___ 2:18
2 Thessalonians
___ 2:8–9

1 Timothy
___ 1:18–20
___ 4:1
___ 5:15
2 Timothy
___ 2:26
James
___ 4:6–7
1 Peter
___ 5:8
2 Peter
___ 2:4

1 John
___ 2:13–14
___ 3:10
___ 4:4
___ 5:18
Jude
___ 6
Revelation
___ 2:9–10, 13
___ 12:11

4 SURVEY ENEMY TERRITORY

Objectives: Through this strategy session, you will learn to:

- Define *the world*
- Identify the prince of the world
- Describe the present condition of the world
- Summarize the structure of the world
- Explain how to overcome the world
- Explain the relationship of the spirit to the flesh
- Identify two categories of people in our world
- Define *the lust of the flesh*
- Define *the lust of the eyes*
- Explain how lust develops
- Explain the results of lust
- Define *the pride of life*

Key Verses for This Study:

> Do not love the world or the things in the world. If anyone loves the world, the love of the Father is not in him. For all that is in the world—the lust of the flesh, the lust of the eyes, and the pride of life—is not of the Father but is of the world. (1 John 2:15–16)

> Now is the judgment of this world; now the ruler of this world will be cast out. (John 12:31)

Step Four: Survey Enemy Territory

Our blessed Savior and his Apostles are wholly taken up in doctrines that relate to common life. They call us to renounce the world, and differ in every temper and way of life, from the spirit and the way of the world: to renounce all its goods, to fear none of its evils, to reject its joys, and have no value for its happiness: to be as new-born babes, that are born into a new state of things: to live as pilgrims in spiritual watchings, in holy fear, and heavenly aspiring after another life: to take up our daily cross, to deny ourselves, to profess the blessedness of mourning, to seek the blessedness of poverty of spirit: to forsake the pride and vanity of riches, to take no thought for the morrow, to live in the profoundest state of humility, to rejoice in worldly sufferings: to reject the lust of the flesh, the lust of the eyes, and the pride of life: to bear injuries, to forgive and bless our enemies, and to love mankind as God loveth them: to give up our whole hearts and affections to God, and strive to enter through the strait gate into a life of eternal glory.
—*William Law*

The prince of demons can only be in one place at a time. Because of this, Satan uses a mighty force of demons who work through the world and the flesh to carry out his evil designs.

Definition of the World

On the night of his betrayal and arrest, Jesus prayed to God concerning His followers. He said, "I have given them Your word; and the world has hated them because they are not of the world, just as I am not of the world" (John 17:14).

Paul told the church, "And do not be conformed to this world, but be transformed by the renewing of your mind . . ." (Rom. 12:2).

Do not confuse this world to which we should not conform with the physical planet earth. God loves the world, the people who dwell here (John 3:16).

The world that Jesus and Paul warn against is our social system, which incorporates all of our beliefs which are contrary to God, and the expressions of those beliefs. This world involves art, music, politics, spiritual matters, science, philosophy, and all other aspects of life contrived without God's input. This system, which runs the inhabited earth, is opposed to God and the Lord Jesus Christ.

The Prince of the World

Satan is the prince or ruler of the world system. "Now is the judgment of this world; now the ruler of this world will be cast out" (John 12:31). "I will no longer talk much with you, for the ruler of this world is coming, and he has nothing in Me" (John 14:30). Satan is also called the god of this age. "Whose minds the god of this age has blinded, who do not believe, lest the light of the gospel of the glory of Christ, who is the image of God, should shine on them" (2 Cor. 4:4).

Look at today's newspaper. Can you identify some events that reveal Satan as the ruler or god of this world? List them.

_____

_____

The Present Condition of the World

Sin is the reason for the present condition of the world. When God created Adam and Eve, He gave them dominion over the planet to guide its systems and inhabitants according to the plan of God.

When they disobeyed, they lost their rulership of earth, giving it into Satan's hands.

Jesus Christ came to earth to retrieve our lost dominion. He planned to destroy the works of the devil. Christ's own crucifixion, the payment for our sin, was God's way of beginning the reclamation of the planet and of pronouncing judgment on the spiritual forces of evil.

But Satan's troops continue to fight, influencing men and women for evil. God has placed the responsibility for stopping these forces in the hands of His army on earth—the church—you and me. "Behold, I give you the authority to trample on serpents and scorpions, and over all the power of the enemy, and nothing shall by any means hurt you" (Luke 10:19).

Which of your Christian religious activities are actually helping to stop the forces of evil?

___

Could you readjust your priorities to be more effective? Explain.

___

The World Structure

Its Attitude

The world is God's enemy. "Adulterers and adulteresses! Do you not know that *friendship with the world is enmity with God?* Whoever therefore wants to be a friend of the world makes himself an enemy of God" (James 4:4, italics added).

The world hates you. "If the world hates you, you know that it hated Me before it hated you. If you were of the world, the world would love its own. Yet because you are not of the world, but I chose you out of the world, therefore the world hates you" (John 15:18–19).

The world takes the attitude: "Assert yourself and be first." But God says, "Esteem others better than yourself." The world says, "Hoard your resources to gain wealth." God responds, "Give and you shall receive." The world says, "Strive for position." God replies, "The greatest among you shall be your servant."

Its Condition

Evil is present in our world: "Who gave Himself for our sins, that He might deliver us from this present evil age, according to the will of our God and Father" (Gal. 1:4). There is also deception in the world: "For many deceivers have gone out into the world" (2 John 7).

Its Elements

The elements of the world, the elementary principles that govern it, are the regulations on which the world structure rests. They are different from the principles upon which God builds His kingdom. "Therefore, if you died with Christ from the basic principles of the world, why, as though living in the world, do you subject yourselves to regulations?" (Col. 2:20). "Even so we, when we were children, were in bondage under the elements of the world" (Gal. 4:3). "Beware lest anyone cheat you through philosophy and empty deceit, according to the tradition of men, according to the basic principles of the world, and not according to Christ" (Col. 2:8).

Its Spirit

The spirit of the world opposes the Spirit of God. "Now we have received, not the spirit of the world, but the Spirit who is from

God, that we might know the things that have been freely given to us by God" (1 Cor. 2:12).

Its Philosophy

The philosophy of the world governs how one perceives reality. "Beware lest anyone cheat you through philosophy and empty deceit, according to the tradition of men, according to the basic principles of the world, and not according to Christ" (Col. 2:8).

Its Wisdom

The world has no inherent wisdom. "For the wisdom of this world is foolishness with God" (1 Cor. 3:19).

Its Course

The course of the world, the routine or way in which it runs, is governed by evil. "In which you once walked according to the course of this world, according to the prince of the power of the air, the spirit who now works in the sons of disobedience" (Eph. 2:2).

Its Peace

God offers peace. "Peace, I leave with you, My peace I give to you; not as the world gives do I give to you. Let not your heart be troubled, neither let it be afraid" (John 14:27).

Its Sorrow

"For godly sorrow produces repentance leading to salvation, not to be regretted; but the sorrow of the world produces death" (2 Cor. 7:10).

Its People

Finally, the people in the world can choose to not be of it: "Behold what manner of love the Father has bestowed on us, that we should be called children of God! Therefore the world does not know us, because it did not know Him" (1 John 3:1). "They are of the world. Therefore they speak as of the world, and the world hears them" (1 John 4:5). "Beloved, I beg you as sojourners and pilgrims, abstain from fleshly lusts which war against the soul" (1 Peter 2:11).

The world's evil force, dominated by Satan, works from the outside to attack believers. It is often veiled in individuals who do not know God.

Although the world is opposed to God, many of its laws and ordinances came from Him. The world still subscribes to a certain moral law to a limited degree and advocates laws that protect people. Government is from the Lord, thus we have a God-given obligation to abide by the laws of the land as long as they are not in direct conflict with the Word of God.

What things in your life entice you toward the world?

Has the enemy ever made you feel that by giving up worldly things you would be forced to live a miserable existence? Looking back now, was Satan telling the truth?

Overcoming the World

We cannot overcome the world or any problem in life through our own strength, but rather through the strength of Him in whom we have placed our faith. We must rely on "Who is he who overcomes the world, but he who believes that Jesus is the Son of God" (1 John 5:5).

To overcome the world we must think differently from the world. "And do not be conformed to this world, but be transformed by the renewing of your mind" (Rom. 12:2).

Examine your attitude toward the world. Can you identify those things that violate a Christian lifestyle and avoid them without condemning everybody and everything in the process? Can you shun evil without developing a negative and pessimistic attitude?

List three areas that need attention in your life.

List steps you need to take to gain victory in these areas.

The Relationship of the Spirit to the Flesh

When we are saved, the Holy Spirit indwells our spirit and begins to move us toward opposing the desires of the flesh. He helps us resist former patterns of overindulgence in yielding to the body.

The flesh rebels against our spirit and the Spirit of God within us. It entices us toward sinful activities. Paul the apostle spoke of the resulting dilemma: "For I know that in me (that is, in my flesh) nothing good dwells; for to will is present with me, but how to perform what is good I do not find. For the good that I will to do, I do not do; but the evil I will not to do, that I practice" (Rom. 7:18–19).

Paul acknowledged that the soul stands between what we know to be right in our spirit and what our bodies (senses) tell us to do. Here in this middle ground, he felt a strong pull from each side. When we are out of fellowship with God, our soul often ends up going the wrong direction because it is used to cooperating with the body under the influence of the old nature. The term *flesh* refers to the soul's cooperation with the body to the exclusion of the spirit. When the soul cooperates with the Spirit of God living in our spirit, giving the body only what it rightfully needs, we become spiritual. The following chart distinguishes between natural humans and spiritual humans.

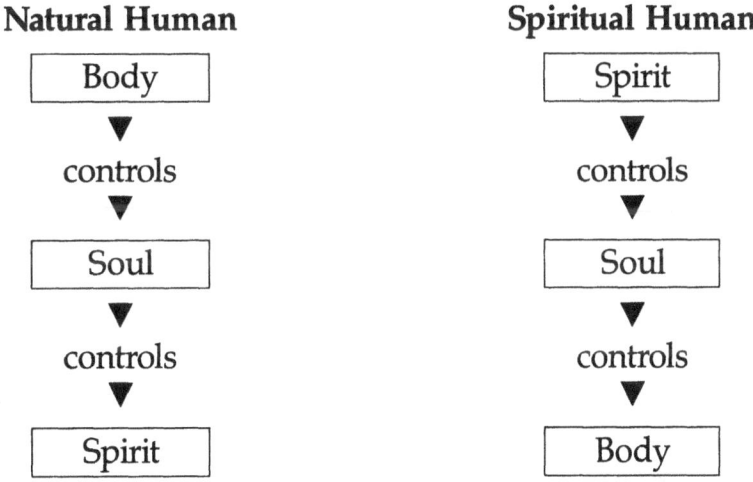

Paul went on to say that he did not do wrong himself but, rather, "sin living in me . . . does it" (Rom. 7:20 NIV), forcing him into bondage. His inner struggle prevented him from doing the good that he desired to do. We often face this same inner struggle—two forces pulling in two different directions. Although it seems logical to blame sin for our problems, God still holds us responsible for the actions produced by that sin. "The soul who sins shall die" (Ezek. 18:20).

At the end of Romans 7 it almost appears that Paul said that since the body has such strength, he should let it do what it wants and just obey his spirit with his mind, not his body. But this is not possible. The body and the spirit cannot both have control. One or the other must govern.

Paul exhorts us to "cast off the works of darkness, and let us put on the armor of light. Let us walk properly, as in the day, not in revelry and drunkenness, not in lewdness and lust, not in strife and envy. But put on the Lord Jesus Christ, and make no provision for the flesh, to fulfill its lusts" (Rom. 13:12-14).

The only way we can allow the spirit to control us and put aside the evil deeds produced by unrestrained body senses is in Jesus Christ. Christ's Spirit, living and dwelling in us, will turn us upside down—or really, right side up—until spirit controls soul and soul controls body. Old things, including our old Adamic nature, pass away and all things become new (2 Cor. 5:17). The human spirit once again becomes dominant as it was before Adam and Eve sinned and is positioned for communication with God.

The following chart illustrates the two categories of people in our world. Adamic humans are controlled by the old nature, the body, and the soul. Christlike humans are controlled by the new nature, the spirit of God, and their own spirits rather than their souls:

Two Categories of People in Our World

Adamic Humans Are Controlled By:	Christlike Humans Are Controlled By
The Old Nature	The New Nature
The body (senses)	The Spirit of God

Adamic Humans Are Controlled By	Christlike Humans Are Controlled By
The soul (will, mind, and emotions)	The spirit of man

The Old Nature	The New Nature
Hates God	Loves God through Jesus
Hates God's people	Loves brothers and sisters in Christ
Does not believe in eternal consequences	Waits for resurrection unto eternal life
Worships self	Worships God
Believes the Bible is only a book	Believes the Bible to be the Word of God

We may choose to let our spirit be in control rather than our body, but without God's help we will not have sufficient power to carry out that desire. When God saves us, He does not want to dominate us and remove our free will. He wants to help us establish control in our spirit so that we have power and knowledge to make correct choices.

This is why Paul's teaching on "Christ in you" is so important. Christ's Spirit strengthens our spirit to place us in control of ourselves. He does this, however, only with our willing cooperation. He does not want to make us slaves to His will.

The Lust of the Flesh

Lust, a desire for overindulgence of a legitimate need, expresses itself in the incessant demand for fulfillment in an abnormal way. It eventually destroys the body, soul, and spirit. The Bible warns that we should not lust after evil things. The consequences of evil experienced by Israel serve as warnings for us. "Now these things became our examples, to the intent that we should not lust after evil things as they also lusted" (1 Cor. 10:6).

The Bible calls lusting after evil things that will please our fleshly nature "lust of the flesh." It involves giving the body what it wants, always gratifying its senses, without regard to what is normal and right.

The Lust of the Eyes

Of the five senses, the eyes seem to be the strongest and the most prone to sin. The Bible warns specifically about the lust of the eyes, which refers to the fleshly temptations that enter our spirit through sight. What we see inscribes almost indelible images on the mind. If they are wrong, they become like leeches fastened to their prey.

In order to keep from sinning with his eyes Job said, "I have made a covenant with my eyes; Why then should I look upon a young woman?" (Job 31:1). And the psalmist prayed: "Turn away my eyes from looking at worthless things" (Ps. 119:37).

How Lust Develops

Lust enters us through the natural senses. Our eyes see and ears hear in order to fulfill legitimate needs of the body and soul. But when the body uses any of the senses to get more than it rightfully needs, it follows the course of sin. Our senses need to become acquainted with the rightful fulfillment of the needs of both body and soul: "But solid food belongs to those who are of full age, that is, those who by reason of use have their senses exercised to discern both good and evil" (Heb. 5:14).

A touch, a taste, or even a smell can foster lust. Satan uses the environment of the world to tempt the flesh.

In and of themselves our senses are not evil, but they can trigger an evil thought or desire. A lustful thought tempts us to do evil: "Let no one say when he is tempted, 'I am tempted by God'; for God cannot be tempted by evil, nor does He Himself tempt anyone" (James 1:13-14).

Remember, God never tempts us. We are tempted when we are drawn away by our own sinful, fleshly desires. But we do not have to yield to this temptation. God always provides a way of escape: "No temptation has overtaken you except such as is common to man; but God is faithful, who will not allow you to be tempted beyond what you are able, but with the temptation will also make the way of escape, that you may be able to bear it" (1 Cor. 10:13).

John also notes that we can no longer be forced to sin as we were before we were saved. "We know that whoever is born of God does not sin; but he who has been born of God keeps himself, and the wicked one does not touch him" (1 John 5:18). That does not mean that we will never again sin. It means that we do not have to sin if we do not want to do so.

We read that "the Scripture has confined all under sin" (Gal. 3:22). Christ has conquered sin, and it has no hold on Him. If we belong to Him it likewise has no hold on us.

Since the mind is used to tempt the flesh, Paul warns, "Because the carnal mind is enmity against God; for it is not subject to the law of God, nor indeed can be. So then, those who are in the flesh cannot please God" (Rom. 8:7-8).

The Results of Lust

Lust leads to sinful actions, called works of the flesh, that cause spiritual death.

Now the works of the flesh are evident, which are: adultery, fornication, uncleanness, lewdness, idolatry, sorcery, hatred, contentions, jealousies, outbursts of wrath, selfish ambitions, dissensions, heresies, envy, murders, drunkenness, revelries, and the like; of which I tell you beforehand, just as I also told you in time past, that those who practice such things will not inherit the kingdom of God. (Gal. 5:19-21)

This list can be divided into different categories of sin:

1. *Sexual sins:* Adultery, fornication, uncleanness, and lewdness
2. *Worship sins:* Idolatry and sorcery
3. *Relationship sins:* Hatred, contention, jealousy, wrath, selfish ambition, dissention, heresy, envy, and murders
4. *Personal sins:* Drunkenness and revelry

Notice how serious these sins are: "those who practice such things will not inherit the kingdom of God." Christians who sometimes find themselves momentarily in sin can free themselves through confession and repentance, but people who "practice" a sinful lifestyle belong to Satan's kingdom.

The world is corrupt because of lust and the resulting works of the flesh: "For the flesh lusts against the Spirit, and the Spirit against the flesh; and these are contrary to one another, so that you do not do the things that you wish" (Gal. 5:17).

> . . . by which have been given to us exceedingly great and precious promises, that through these you may be partakers of the divine nature, having escaped the corruption that is in the world through lust. (2 Peter 1:4)

If you still feel compelled to sin at times, read Romans 6:11-14, where Paul advised us to reckon ourselves dead to sin.

One of the most wonderful aspects of our salvation is its ability to break the power of sin. Paul declared, "For sin shall not have dominion over you" (Rom. 6:14). If a sin plagues you, submit it right now to the power of Christ within you. Realize that according to the Word of God, you do not have to be forced to sin.

Summarize what you have learned about lust.

How does lust develop?

___

What does "lust of the flesh" mean?

___

What does "lust of the eyes" mean?

___

What are the results of lust?

___

The Pride of Life

Our rebellion has created a spirit of independence within us that says we need nothing and no one. We can make it through life on our own. Such arrogance, with its boasting, destroys God's intent for corporate living, including marriage, the family, and the community. "For all that is in the world—the lust of the flesh, the lust of the eyes, and the pride of life—is not of the Father but is of the world" (1 John 2:16).

Read Joshua 6-9. These chapters describe three major battles the nation of Israel fought to claim the promised land, each of which has spiritual significance through what it represents.

The promised land symbolizes the believer's inheritance. The city of Jericho, with all of its charm and allure, represents the world. The city of Ai, with its failure by Achan, can be seen as flesh, and the Gibeonites, with their lies and deceit, represent the devil.

We deal with Jericho (the world) by faith. Israel walked around the walls of the city, and on the seventh day the walls fell down.

We deal with Ai (sins of the flesh) by confession and repentance.

We must exercise caution in dealing with the devil. Joshua did not seek God. He was deceived by the Gibeonites, and he made an alliance with them. This is why we must be aware of the "wiles of the devil" (Eph. 6:11) so we are not "ignorant of his devices" (2 Cor. 2:11).

Do you have an ongoing battle with the world? If so, how might you win this battle by faith?

_____
_____

Are you warring against the flesh? List your weaknesses below, then confess and repent before God.

_____
_____

Have you been deceived by the devil? How? What can you do to combat these situations?

_____
_____

5 MEET THE CAPTAIN OF GOD'S ARMY

Objectives: Through this strategy session, you will learn to:

- Identify the Captain of God's army
- Explain His mission to earth
- Discuss His role in spiritual warfare
- Identify names that reflect His character
- Recognize that angels execute His will

Key Verses for This Study:

> For it was fitting for Him, for whom are all things and by whom are all things, in bringing many sons to glory, to make the captain of their salvation perfect through sufferings. (Heb. 2:10)

> For God so loved the world that He gave His only begotten Son, that whoever believes in Him should not perish but have everlasting life. (John 3:16)

> He who sins is of the devil, for the devil has sinned from the beginning. For this purpose the Son of God was manifested, that He might destroy the works of the devil. (1 John 3:8)

Step Five: Meet the Captain of God's Army

The mark of a life governed by the Holy Spirit is that such a life is continually and ever more and more occupied with Christ, that Christ is becoming greater and greater as time goes on. The effect of the Holy Spirit's work in us is to bring us to the shore of a mighty ocean which reaches far, far beyond our range, and concerning which we feel—Oh, the depths, the fullness, of Christ! If we live as long as ever man lived, we shall still be only on the fringe of this vast fullness that Christ is.
—T. Austin-Sparks

In this chapter we will meet the Captain of the army of God and discover who He is, why He came to earth, what He did, and how He relates to spiritual warfare.

The Captain of God's Army

The Captain of God's army is Jesus Christ. "For it was fitting for Him, for whom are all things and by whom are all things, in bringing many sons to glory, to make the captain of their salvation perfect through sufferings" (Heb. 2:10).

- He is the Creator of all things: "He is the image of the invisible God, the firstborn over all creation. *For by Him all things were created that are in heaven and that are on earth, visible and invisible, whether thrones or dominions or principalities or powers. All things were created through Him and for Him. And He is before all things, and in Him all things consist*" (Col. 1:15–17, italics added).

  And from Hebrews 1:1–2: "God, who at various times and in various ways spoke in time past to the fathers by the prophets, has in these last days spoken to us by His Son, whom He has appointed heir of all things, *through whom also He made the worlds*" (italics added).

- He is the Son of God: ". . . and declared to be the Son of God with power, according to the Spirit of holiness, by the resurrection from the dead" (Rom. 1:4).
- He is God the Son: Jesus is not only the Son of God, He is also God the Son. Paul said Jesus created "all things" (Col. 1:16). But notice that in the Old Testament, Nehemiah said that *God* created all things: "You alone are the Lord; / You have made heaven, / The heaven of heavens, with all their host, / The earth and everything on it, / The seas and all that is in them, / And You preserve them all. / The host of heaven worships You" (Neh. 9:6). Paul claimed that Jesus created everything, and Nehemiah said that God did. Therefore, Jesus must be God.

Another comparison of Scripture indicates the same thing. The writer of Hebrews said, "But when He again brings the firstborn into the world, He says: 'Let all the angels of God worship Him'" (Heb. 1:6). But it was written long ago: "You shall worship the LORD your God, and Him only you shall serve" (Luke 4:8).

If angels were to worship Jesus, and God was the only one to be worshiped, then Jesus must be God.

The early religious Jews wanted to destroy Jesus because He referred to Himself as God and spoke of God as His Father. To a Jew, who was not allowed to speak or write the name of God, it was unthinkable to associate oneself with Him in such intimate terms, "But Jesus answered them, 'My Father has been working until now, and I have been working.' Therefore the Jews sought all the more to kill Him, because He not only broke the Sabbath, but also said that God was His Father, *making Himself equal with God*" (John 5:17–18, italics added).

Such claims by Jesus finally overwhelmed these religious Jews. "Jesus said to them, 'Most assuredly, I say to you, before Abraham was, I AM.' Then they took up stones to throw at Him;

but Jesus hid Himself and went out of the temple, going through the midst of them, and so passed by" (John 8:58–59). The statement "I AM" seems quite harmless, so why all the fuss? These leaders no doubt knew that the expression "I AM" was one of the eternal names of God (see Ex. 3). When Jesus used it, He was openly declaring His deity.

- Jesus is God in human form.

> Who, being in the form of God, did not consider it robbery to be equal with God, but made Himself of no reputation, taking the form of a servant, and coming in the likeness of men. And being found in appearance as a man, He humbled Himself and became obedient to the point of death, even the death of the cross. (Phil. 2:6–8)

> God was manifested in the flesh, / Justified in the Spirit, / Seen by angels, / Preached among the Gentiles, / Believed on in the world, / Received up in glory. (1 Tim. 3:16)

> By this you know the Spirit of God: Every spirit that confesses that Jesus Christ has come in the flesh is of God. (1 John 4:2)

Summarize what you have learned about the identity of the Captain of God's army.

_____

_____

His Mission on Earth

Jesus came to earth to accomplish at least two specific goals. First, *He was sent by the Father to pardon us from sin and restore us to fellowship with God.*

For God so loved the world that He gave His only begotten Son, that whoever believes in Him should not perish but have everlasting life. For God did not send His Son into the world to condemn the world, but that the world through Him might be saved. He who believes in Him is not condemned; but he who does not believe is condemned already, because he has not believed in the name of the only begotten Son of God. (John 3:16–18)

Second, *He came to destroy the works of the devil.* "He who sins is of the devil, for the devil has sinned from the beginning. For this purpose the Son of God was manifested, *that He might destroy the works of the devil*" (1 John 3:8, italics added).

As part of God's plan, Jesus came to earth in human form, ministered among men, died for the sins of man, was resurrected from the dead, and commissioned His followers to bear the gospel of salvation to the nations of the world. The Gospels provide a partial record of Jesus' days on earth.

Summarize the two goals of Jesus during His time on earth.

_____

_____

Jesus' Role in Spiritual Warfare

Jesus ministers in two capacities that relate to the spiritual warfare of the believer.

First, through Him we can claim authority over the enemy. The death of Jesus not only freed us from sin, but it also gave us the power and authority to overcome the world, the flesh, and the devil. "Then He called His twelve disciples together and gave them power and authority over all demons, and to cure diseases" (Luke 9:1).

Second, Jesus intercedes for us, talking to the Father on our behalf, as we engage in spiritual warfare. "It is Christ who died, and furthermore is also risen, who is even at the right hand of God, who also makes intercession for us" (Rom. 8:34).

In what specific areas do you need Jesus to help you triumph over the forces of evil?
_____
_____

What specific things do you want Jesus to intercede for in your behalf?
_____
_____

Take time right now to tell the Lord about the things you have listed.

Names That Reflect Jesus' Character

The following partial list of the names of Jesus recorded in Scripture help us to better understand His character. They can also teach us how to relate to Him as Commander of God's army.

Advocate:	1 John 2:1
Almighty:	Revelation 1:8
Alpha and Omega:	Revelation 21:6
Amen:	Revelation 3:14
Ancient of Days:	Daniel 7:9
Author/Finisher of Our Faith:	Hebrews 12:2
Author of Eternal Salvation:	Hebrews 5:9
Beloved:	Ephesians 1:6
BRANCH:	Zechariah 3:8

Bread of Life:	John 6:48
Bright and Morning Star:	Revelation 22:16
Captain of the Lord's Host:	Joshua 5:15
Carpenter's Son:	Matthew 13:55
Chief Cornerstone:	1 Peter 2:6
Chiefest Among Ten Thousand:	Song of Solomon 5:10
Christ:	John 1:41
Counselor:	Isaiah 9:6
Deliverer:	Romans 11:26
Door:	John 10:9
Elect:	Isaiah 42:1
Eternal Life:	1 John 5:20
Faithful and True:	Revelation 19:11
Faithful Witness:	Revelation 1:5
Firstborn:	Hebrews 1:6
First and Last:	Revelation 22:13
Glorious Lord:	Isaiah 33:21
Great High Priest:	Hebrews 4:14
Head of the Body:	Colossians 1:18
Head Over All Things:	Ephesians 1:22
Headstone:	Psalm 118:22
Heir of All Things:	Hebrews 1:2
Holy One of Israel:	Isaiah 41:14
Hope of Glory:	Colossians 1:27
I AM:	John 8:58
Image of the Invisible God:	Colossians 1:15
Immanuel:	Matthew 1:23
Jesus Christ Our Lord:	Romans 1:3
King of Glory:	Psalm 24:7
Lamb of God:	John 1:29
Light of the World:	John 8:12
Lily of the Valleys:	Song of Solomon 2:1
Living Bread:	John 6:51

Names That Reflect Jesus' Character—Cont'd

Lord God Almighty:	Revelation 4:8
Lord of All:	Acts 10:36
Lord Our Righteousness:	Jeremiah 23:6
Man of Sorrows:	Isaiah 53:3
Master:	Matthew 23:10
Messiah:	Daniel 9:25
Most Holy:	Daniel 9:24
Nazarene:	Matthew 2:23
Only Wise God:	1 Timothy 1:17
Our Passover:	1 Corinthians 5:7
Physician:	Luke 4:23
Prince of Peace:	Isaiah 9:6
Propitiation:	Romans 3:25
Redeemer:	Isaiah 59:20
Resurrection:	John 11:25
Righteous Servant:	Isaiah 53:11
Root of Jesse:	Isaiah 11:10
Rose of Sharon:	Song of Solomon 2:1
Savior of the World:	1 John 4:14
Seed of David:	John 7:42
Seed of the Woman:	Genesis 3:15
Shepherd:	John 10:11
Son of God:	Romans 1:4
Son of Man:	Acts 7:56
Son of Mary:	Mark 6:3
Stone:	Matthew 21:42
Sun of Righteousness:	Malachi 4:2
Sure Foundation:	Isaiah 28:16
Teacher:	John 3:2
Truth:	John 14:6
Unspeakable Gift:	2 Corinthians 9:15
Vine:	John 15:1

Way:	John 14:6
Wonderful:	Isaiah 9:6
Word:	John 1:14
Word of God:	Revelation 19:13

Which of these names are most important in spiritual warfare?
_____
_____

Which names describe your relationship to the Lord?
_____
_____

Which names reveal the deity and glory of Jesus?
_____
_____

Which *one* name of Jesus has been most significant to you in your Christian experience?
_____

During the next few days, take time to study the Bible references provided for each name.

Angels Execute God's Will

Angel means "messenger" and in different circumstances can refer to both humans and other unique creations of God. An angel may be one of the "sons of God" (Job 1:6) or people such as prophets and pastors (Rev. 2:1; 3:14). Although we have limited knowledge of angels, there are several things we do know about them:

- They are created beings: Ephesians 3:9; Colossians 1:16
- They talk, eat, etc.: Psalm 78:25
- They take charge in the affairs of people: Genesis 19:1, 15; Hebrews 1:14
- They are not to be worshiped: Colossians 2:18
- They will be judged by people: 1 Corinthians 6:3
- They come in large companies: Psalm 68:17; Matthew 26:53
- Some are good: Luke 9:26
- Some are bad: Matthew 25:41
- There are different kinds, i.e. seraphim, cherubim, archangel: Genesis 3:24; Isaiah 6:2, 6; Ezekiel 10:15–16; 1 Thessalonians 4:16; Jude 9
- They are in ranks: Ephesians 6:12; Revelation 12:7

Study each of the references about angels. Summarize what they teach us:

_____
_____
_____

6 COMPLETE BASIC TRAINING

Objectives: Through this strategy session, you will learn to:

- Develop a wartime lifestyle
- Receive your commission to fight
- Fight until you overcome
- Know the objectives of spiritual warfare
- Master basic training
- Recognize types of attacks
- Communicate with the Captain through prayer
- Understand the importance of the warfare manual (the Bible)
- Work with the troops
- Know your weapons

Key Verses for This Study:

> To him who overcomes I will give to eat from the tree of life, which is in the midst of the Paradise of God. (Rev. 2:7)

> I have fought the good fight, I have finished the race, I have kept the faith. (2 Tim. 4:7)

Step Six: Complete Basic Training

Many people have joined God's army, but some have not taken the Scriptures about spiritual warfare seriously and therefore have not gone forth to fight. They may say such things as, "What can I do?" or "God has already defeated the enemy, all we need to do is sit and wait for His return" or "If God wanted me to fight, He would tell me to do so."

God wants us to join Him in finishing the battle against Satan and his demons to gain on-the-job training for ruling with Him in His marvelous universe. But in order to be effective in this battle, we must adopt a wartime lifestyle, receive basic training in spiritual warfare, and learn to overcome.

A Wartime Lifestyle

General Charles James Gordon, the hero of Khartoum, was a truly Christian soldier. Shut up in the Sudanese town he gallantly held out for one year, but, finally, was overcome and slain. On his memorial in Westminster Abbey are these words, "He gave his money to the poor; his sympathy to the sorrowing; his life to his country and his soul to God."

—*Homer W. Hodge*

When a nation goes to war, the manner and style in which its people live is greatly affected. People give up jobs and spend hours in preparation, training extensively for combat. Funds are withdrawn from the economy to aid in the battle. Residents become aware of the potential of invasion, and extra guards are posted at national borders.

We are at war!

We must adopt a spiritual wartime lifestyle if we are to be obedient to Christ. Spiritual warfare must become a primary focus of our lives. We must prepare and train. We must learn to use our spiritual weapons. We must be alert to enemy invasion and post extra guards at the borders of our heart, mind, tongue, soul, spirit, home, community, and church fellowship. Our lifestyle must reflect the fact that we are at war.

Commissioned to Fight

Jesus waged war against the enemy and then told us to do the same. "Behold, I give you the authority to trample on serpents and scorpions, and over all the power of the enemy, and nothing shall by any means hurt you" (Luke 10:19).

Paul also confirms the fight at hand: "I have fought the good fight, I have finished the race, I have kept the faith" (2 Tim. 4:7).

Describe the kind of power we have over the enemy.

_____

_____

Fighting Until You Overcome

The goal of this warfare is not to win a few isolated skirmishes but to fight and overcome continuously until the end of life on this earth. Although God does not expect us to battle or overcome in our own strength, He does expect us to fight under His leadership and guidance and with His power and authority.

The Overcomer's Example

Jesus overcame the world. "These things I have spoken to you, that in Me you may have peace. In the world you will have tribulation; but be of good cheer, I have overcome the world" (John 16:33).

The Overcomer's Method

Because the Holy Spirit lives in us, we can overcome Satan's forces. "You are of God, little children, and have overcome them, because He who is in you is greater than he who is in the world" (1 John 4:4). We overcome by the new birth experience and our faith. "For whatever is born of God overcomes the world. And this is the victory that has overcome the world—our faith. Who is he who overcomes the world, but he who believes that Jesus is the Son of God?" (1 John 5:4–5). And we overcome by the blood of Jesus and our testimony. "And they overcame him by the blood of the Lamb and by the word of their testimony, and they did not love their lives to the death" (Rev. 12:11).

The Overcomer's Promises

Scripture makes some beautiful promises, to those who win this spiritual battle. Overcomers will . . .

Eat of the tree of life: Revelation 2:7
Eat of hidden manna: Revelation 2:17
Be clothed in white raiment: Revelation 3:5
Be pillars in the temple of God: Revelation 3:12
Sit with Jesus on His throne: Revelation 3:21
Have a new name: Revelation 2:17
Have power over the nations: Revelation 2:26
Have the name of God written upon them: Revelation 3:12
Have a special relationship with God: Revelation 21:7
Have the Morning Star (Jesus): Revelation 2:28
Be confessed by Jesus before God the Father: Revelation 3:5
Not be hurt by the second death: Revelation 2:11

Not have their names blotted out of the Book of Life: Revelation 3:5

Inherit all things: Revelation 21:7

What do these verses teach about the overcomer's example?
_____
_____

What do they reveal about the overcomer's method?
_____
_____

What have you learned about the overcomer's promises?
_____
_____

Knowing the Objectives

In order to overcome evil we must understand the objective of spiritual warfare which is to bring all things under the authority of Jesus Christ. To achieve this, we must win individual victories over the enemy under Christ's leadership.

We achieve victory in natural warfare by winning many short-range objectives—individual battles won and specific territories claimed. Each of these individual battles contributes to the final goal of victory.

The same is true in the spirit world. Our long-range goal is total victory over the enemy. But we must see this long-range objective in terms of short-range goals.

Here are some personal objectives you may want to set:

I. To be personally pleasing to the Lord.
   (A) Attitude
   (B) Speech
   (C) Lifestyle

II. To find God's will.
   (A) His will for all mankind
   (B) His will for you personally

III. To love others.
   (A) Learn to give
   (B) Learn to receive

IV. To prepare for spiritual battle.
   (A) Put on armor of God
   (B) Identify weapons with which to fight the enemy

Can you think of other personal warfare objectives you should set? If so, list them.

_____

_____

Basic Training

Sending soldiers to the battlefield without basic training would result in defeat. When soldiers enter basic training, they leave civilian life behind. They are no longer entangled with civilian affairs but are concerned with the army in which they have enlisted.

In the spiritual battle, in order to wage a good war, we must likewise not be entangled in the affairs of this life. We must focus on eternal things, rather than on temporal matters. This present life is transitory. We are not citizens of this world, and certainly not civilians. We are warriors in the kingdom of God. "You therefore must endure hardship as a good soldier of Jesus Christ. No one engaged in warfare entangles himself with the affairs of this life, that he may please him who enlisted him as a soldier" (2 Tim. 2:3–4).

There are three primary areas of basic training:

1. Increasing in knowledge and application of the Word.
2. Developing a prayer life.
3. Learning to interact with other members of the body of Christ.

Evaluate yourself on each of these:

How well do I understand and apply the Word?

_____
_____

Do I have a well-developed prayer life?

_____
_____

How well do I interact with other members of the body of Christ?

_____
_____

Types of Attacks

The principle of "attack and counterattack" is crucial in defeating the enemy. When one side attacks, the other side counterattacks. A counterattack keeps the aggressor from advancing or regaining lost territory.

Satan counterattacks offensive moves made by believers. When we decide to pray more, study the Word of God, or engage in ministry, he will immediately stage a counterattack to prevent us from advancing. If we are aware of this strategy, we will be prepared, not caught off guard.

For example, a young man may feel a call to the ministry and be asked to teach a Sunday school class in his church. As he considers the task, he suddenly remembers a sin committed long ago. Even though the sin had been confessed, he feels unworthy of the assignment and is tempted to decline. Not until he discovers there is no condemnation in Jesus and he is free from his past because of the blood of Jesus does he find release to accept the assignment.

Recall a time in which you were moving to a new level of spiritual maturity and try to remember what problems you faced. How did those problems affect what God was doing in your life?

_____

_____

What did you do to counter Satan's attack? _____

_____

Military terms identify three kinds of enemy attacks:

1. *Frontal attack:* Direct attacks often involve temptation and accusation. They force a person to make an immediate decision as illustrated in the temptation of Jesus, when Satan encouraged Him to turn stones to bread, jump from the pinnacle of the temple, and give allegiance to Satan.
2. *Siege or blockade:* In a siege or blockade, the enemy takes control of new territory. Consistent failure and giving in to

temptation, as in addiction to drugs or alcohol, can lead to a siege or blockade. The enemy breaks into our spiritual existence and gains control of a part of our life. The enemy does not actually possess the area, but he prevents us from functioning properly for God's glory.
3. *Invasion and occupation:* This occurs when the enemy (a demon) finds an open door (drugs, the occult, false religion) and no resistance to his entering. He sometimes can gain such forceful control that the person involved is said to be "demon possessed." The Gadarene demoniac is an example of such powerful control (Luke 8:26–36).

Have you ever experienced any of these types of attacks in your spiritual life? What happened? How did you respond? How could you have improved your response to the attack?

Type of Attack	What Happened	How I Responded
Frontal attack		
Siege or blockade		
Invasion and occupation		

Communicating with the Captain: Prayer

"Prayer concerns conduct and conduct makes character. Conduct is what we do; character is what we are. Conduct is outward life. Character is the life unseen, hidden within, yet evidenced by that which *is* seen. Conduct is external, seen from without; character is internal—operating within. In the economy of grace conduct is the offspring of character. Character is the state of the heart, conduct its outward expression. Character is the root of the tree, conduct, the fruit it bears."[1]

No soldier can fight effectively without prayer. We must pursue an understanding of prayer, our greatest source of power, if we are to overcome. We have included a list of recommended books on prayer in the notes for this chapter at the end of the book.[2]

A soldier cannot train adequately for warfare without communicating with his leaders. Christian warriors must also communicate with their Captain to be victorious in battle. This is done through prayer.

Prayer has been defined as "any thought turned heavenward." Prayer is also praise, worship, singing to God, meditation, thanksgiving, listening, silence, waiting on the Lord, and confession. These are important and vitally necessary, but of all the kinds of prayer, intercession gives the warring soldier fighting power. "Therefore I exhort first of all that supplications, prayers, intercessions, and giving of thanks be made for all men, for kings and all who are in authority, that we may lead a quiet and peaceable life in all godliness and reverence" (1 Tim. 2:1–2).

Intercession, in part, is an element of warfare. In practice, it is praying for others. In reality, it is warfare praying; it is violent praying. At times it is marching into enemy territory and taking ground from the enemy. "And from the days of John the Baptist until now the kingdom of heaven suffers violence, and the violent take it by force" (Matt. 11:12).

An intercessor is one who takes the place of others or pleads their cause. When we intercede, we stand before God and between the enemy and the person for whom we are praying. We do so by the authority vested in us by Jesus Christ. In intercession, we command demon spirits to release their hold on individuals and the circumstances and situations surrounding them.

Hindrances to Prayer

Here are some attitudes and actions that hinder effective prayer:

Wrong motives and requests: James 4:2–3
Sin of any kind: Isaiah 59:1–2
Idols in the heart: Ezekiel 14:1–3
An unforgiving spirit: Mark 11:25
Selfishness: Proverbs 21:13
Mistreatment of family members: 1 Peter 3:7
Self-righteousness: Luke 18:10–14
Unbelief: James 1:6–7
Failure to abide in Christ and His Word: John 15:7

Of all the hindrances to prayer, one of the greatest is lack of commitment. Until we commit ourselves to prayer, we will not win the battle.

Have you experienced any of these hindrances in prayer? What could you do to remove the hindrance?

Hindrance	How I Can Remove This Hindrance
Wrong motives and requests	_____
Sin	_____
Idols in the heart	_____
An unforgiving spirit	_____
Selfishness	_____
Mistreatment of family members	_____
Self-righteousness	_____
Unbelief	_____
Failure to abide in Christ and His Word	_____
Lack of commitment	_____

Intercession requires the help of the Holy Spirit. In this, the highest element of prayer, God's Spirit gives breath to our prayers.

"Likewise the Spirit also helps in our weaknesses. For we do not know what we should pray for as we ought, but the Spirit Himself makes intercession for us with groanings which cannot be uttered" (Rom. 8:26).

To learn to intercede, we must get to know our Captain. The apostle Paul said, "that I may know Him and the power of His resurrection, and the fellowship of His sufferings, being conformed to His death" (Phil. 3:10).

The enemy tries to hinder communication between the troops and their leader. He works to stop prayer and the reading of God's Word. This results in confusion on the battlefield. If we neglect the basic means of communication with the Captain, the enemy can easily defeat us.

As we receive God's instructions, we must obey them. Soldiers in the natural world must follow orders from those in charge. The same is true in the spiritual realm. To fight effectively, we must follow the instructions of our Captain. We must learn obedience to the communication received from Him through His Word.

Pray the Promises

God answers prayer according to His promises. When we do not pray on the basis of these promises, He will not answer our prayer. "You ask and do not receive, because you ask amiss, that you may spend it on your pleasures" (James 4:3). No parents promise to give their child anything he wants or asks for. Parents make it clear that they will do certain things, but not others. Within limits, they answer their child's requests. Likewise, God answers our prayers within the limits of His promises.

Scriptural Guidelines for Prayer

Look up and study the following scriptural guidelines for prayer.

Pray repeatedly but without empty repetition: Daniel 6:10; Matthew 6:7; Luke 11:5-13; Luke 18:1-8

Pray for others without fail: 1 Samuel 12:23

Pray with understanding: Ephesians 6:18

Pray in the Spirit: Romans 8:26; Jude 20

Pray according to the will of God: 1 John 5:14-15

Pray in secret: Matthew 6:6

Pray stressing quality rather than quantity. Prayer is not successful because of "much speaking": Matthew 6:7

Pray always: Luke 21:35; Ephesians 6:18

Pray continually: Romans 12:12

Pray without ceasing: 1 Thessalonians 5:17

Pray to the Father in the name of Jesus: John 15:16

Pray with a watchful attitude: 1 Peter 4:7

Pray according to the example of the model prayer: Matthew 6:9-13

Pray with a forgiving spirit: Mark 11:25

Pray and fast at times: Matthew 17:21

Pray fervently: James 5:16; Colossians 4:12

Pray in submission to God: Luke 22:42

Pray using the strategies of binding and loosing: Matthew 16:19

Pray that you enter not into temptation: Luke 22:40-46

Pray for them that despitefully use you (your enemies): Luke 6:28

Pray for all the saints: Ephesians 6:18

Pray for the sick: James 5:14

Pray one for another (bearing each other's burdens): James 5:16

Pray for all men, kings, and those in authority: 1 Timothy 2:1-4

Pray for your daily needs to be supplied: Matthew 6:11

Pray for wisdom: James 1:5

Pray for healing: James 5:14-15

Pray for forgiveness: Matthew 6:12

Pray for God's will and kingdom to be established: Matthew 6:10

Pray for relief from affliction: James 5:13

The Warfare Manual: God's Word

In basic training we must learn to understand God's battle plan as revealed in His Word. Here, we discover how to put on the armor of God. We discover weapons such as the blood of the Lamb, the

Word of our testimony, the name of Jesus, praise, singing, and intercession and how to use them. We also learn how to "cast down imaginations" and how to "bring into captivity every thought to the obedience of Christ." Understanding His Word is vital for effective warfare.

> Your word is a lamp to my feet
> And a light to my path. (Ps. 119:105)

> The entrance of Your words gives light;
> It gives understanding to the simple. (Ps. 119:130)

In meeting the temptations of Satan, Jesus used the Word of God. He quoted specific Scriptures applicable to the immediate battle. In order to use the Word of God effectively in spiritual warfare, we must know not only what it says, but also what it means. We must study it, meditate on it, and memorize it. Many defeats in life come because we do not know and understand God's Word. "Jesus answered and said to them, 'You are mistaken, not knowing the Scriptures nor the power of God'" (Matt. 22:29).

Working with the Troops

Basic training also includes instruction in how to cooperate with other soldiers. Although God has many troops, He has only one army. Each believer enters God's army as a private and has a relationship to all other soldiers. Contrary to what some believe, God does not have sixty million armies with one person in each army.

> For in fact the body is not one member but many. If the foot should say, "Because I am not a hand, I am not of the body," is it therefore not of the body? And if the ear should say, "Because I am not an eye, I am not of the body," is it therefore not of the

body? If the whole body were an eye, where would be the hearing? If the whole were hearing, where would be the smelling? But now God has set the members, each one of them, in the body just as He pleased. And if they were all one member, where would the body be? But now indeed there are many members, yet one body. And the eye cannot say to the hand, "I have no need of you"; nor again the head to the feet, "I have no need of you." (1 Cor. 12:14-21)

A teachable soldier grows, matures, and gains greater degrees of usefulness and effectiveness. As fellow soldiers, we have a responsibility to protect each other. Negativism, bitterness, and criticism are Satan's strategies for defeating us from within.

Satan also leads numbers of soldiers astray through isolationism, factions, envies, jealousies, hatred, selfish ambitions, and other kinds of discord. He tries to destroy teamwork by instilling a lust for power that creates an army with all leaders and no followers. Like every other army, God's army has an organizational structure:

And He Himself gave some to be apostles, some prophets, some evangelists, and some pastors and teachers, for the equipping of the saints for the work of ministry, for the edifying of the body of Christ, till we all come to the unity of the faith and the knowledge of the Son of God, to a perfect man, to the measure of the stature of the fullness of Christ. (Eph. 4:11-13)

Let every soul be subject to the governing authorities. For there is no authority except from God, and the authorities that exist are appointed by God. Therefore whoever resists the authority resists the ordinance of God, and those who resist will bring judgment on themselves. (Rom. 13:1-2)

Spiritual warfare is a team effort. Soldiers must cooperate with one another in order to defeat the enemy. They must follow the direction of their Commander (Jesus) and those to whom He has delegated authority within the church. They must move forward as a united front.

In the natural world, when a soldier is wounded, his companions make heroic rescue efforts. They do not leave the weak behind, but place them under protection until they recover from their wounds. This, however, is not always the case in the Christian army.

As one Christian leader suggests, the Christian army tends to "shoot its wounded." When believers fall in battle, we frequently view them with contempt. We are quick to place blame, find fault, and condemn. Often the wounded are surrendered to the enemy. Instead, we should rescue these individuals and surround them with our strength.

What does Paul say we should do to the repentant sinner (see Eph. 4:32)?

_____

What should we do for other members of Christ's body (see James 5:16)?

_____

What about Weapons?

Every war has weapons. They may be simple (a spear or bow and arrow) or complex (a missile system). In God's army, our weapons are spiritual. "For the weapons of our warfare are not carnal but mighty in God for pulling down strongholds, casting down arguments and every high thing that exalts itself against the knowledge of God, bringing every thought into captivity to the obedience of Christ" (2 Cor. 10:4–5).

Christian soldiers must know how to use the weapons available to them. Some weapons are specifically designed for defense while others are for offense. In the next two chapters we will learn about these weapons.

Part Four
MOBILIZATION

ACTIVE MILITARY SERVICE IN GOD'S ARMY

To *mobilize* means "to put in a state of readiness for active military service." Mobilization is the process of being deployed as part of God's army.

In this section you will learn to arm yourself with both defensive and offensive weapons and to employ offensive and defensive strategies in spiritual warfare.

7 ARM YOURSELF WITH DEFENSIVE WEAPONS

Objectives: Through this strategy session, you will learn to:

- Make personal preparations for power by gaining knowledge of God's Word, resisting the sins of the flesh, relinquishing the cares of this life, and conquering spiritual pride.
- Arm yourself with defensive weapons, including the belt of truth, the breastplate of righteousness, the preparation of the gospel, the shield of faith, the helmet of salvation, and the sword of the Spirit.

Key Verses for This Study:

Finally, my brethren, be strong in the Lord and in the power of His might. Put on the whole armor of God, that you may be able to stand against the wiles of the devil. (Eph. 6:10–11)

Fight the good fight of faith, lay hold on eternal life, to which you were also called and have confessed the good confession in the presence of many witnesses. (1 Tim. 6:12)

Step Seven: Arm Yourself with Defensive Weapons

Quite often Christian experience founders on the rock of conduct. Beautiful theories are marred by ugly lives. The most

difficult thing about piety, as it is the most impressive, is to be able to live it. It is the life which counts, and our praying suffers, as do other phases of our religious experience, from bad living.
—E. M. Bounds

In the previous chapter we discussed basic training for spiritual battle. In this chapter we will look at the power we have for overcoming Satan's demons and the defensive weapons God makes available for waging effective warfare.

Preparations for Power

Victory that comes as a result of the manifestation of God's power, as well as any other blessing from Him, is conditional. We must follow certain steps in order for God to fulfill His promises. These steps are usually simple for those who are sincere about their relationship with the Lord. Let's take a brief look at four things that are basic to defense in spiritual warfare.

1. *Gaining knowledge of God's Word.* In warfare, ignorance of the enemy can lead to defeat. How can any army operate effectively if it doesn't know the tactics of those it opposes? The apostle Paul fought Satan effectively and offered this reason for his success: ". . . for we are not ignorant of his devices" (2 Cor. 2:11).

Evidently Paul never took Satan for granted. No doubt he searched for ways to understand the demonic realm. He did not become preoccupied with it, but he certainly became aware of it in order not to be deceived.

Charles Swindoll cautions:

Before any opponent can be intelligently withstood, a knowledge of his ways must be known. Ignorance must be dispelled. No boxer in his right mind enters the ring without having first studied the other boxer's style. The same is true on the football field. Or the battlefield. Days (sometimes *months*) are spent studying the tactics, the weaknesses, the strengths of the opponent. Ignorance is an enemy to victory.[1]

While some tragically dwell too much on themes related to Satan and demons, many have the idea that just "being a Christian" is good enough. "Since you belong to God, sit back and relax. He will take care of you. After all, God will put a hedge around you so that Satan can't get through. Forget Satan. He'll go away. Just don't talk about him." But this is exactly what the enemy desires. Is it any wonder that some Christians are overcome? God said, "My people are destroyed for lack of knowledge" (Hosea 4:6).

Beware also of the mistaken idea that we should not know too much of the Word of God because "the less we know the less we will held be accountable for." We will be held accountable not only for what we know but also for what we could have known.

2. *Resisting the sins of the flesh.* Sin causes separation from God. It allows Satan to gain influence and sometimes even control. Sin hinders our power to combat the Evil One, especially when it is a known sin. "Therefore, to him who knows to do good and does not do it, to him it is sin" (James 4:17). Indulging in the sins of the flesh, as recorded in Galatians 5:19-21, inhibits God's power.

All people, including Christians, sin. That is why God provided a solution (see 1 John 1:9). As Christians, we are not to live in bondage to sin. We have been set free. Neither are we to assume that the grace of God allows us to live any way we please once we are saved. "What shall we say then? Shall we continue in sin that grace may abound? Certainly not! How shall we who died to sin live any longer in it?" (Rom. 6:1-2).

When Jesus confronted the adulteress He told her to "go and sin no more" (John 8:11).

The writer of Hebrews told his readers to "lay aside every weight, and the sin which so easily ensnares us" (Heb. 12:1).

Paul told the Corinthians to "flee sexual immorality" (1 Cor. 6:18). They were also warned to "flee from idolatry" (1 Cor. 10:14).

Paul commanded Timothy to "flee these things and pursue righteousness, godliness, faith, love, patience, gentleness" (1 Tim. 6:11). This admonition reveals that it is not enough just to forsake sin. We must substitute in its place righteousness, faith, love, and peace.

3. *Relinquishing the cares of this life.* Because we are engaged in a spiritual war, it is essential to give undivided attention to the Captain of our salvation. As most soldiers know, at times we must occasionally put aside some of the good and legitimate pleasures of life to assure victory. This does not mean that we must live depressed or poverty-stricken lives. Nor does it mean we cannot enjoy life or experience pleasure. It simply means we must make sacrifices in order to win battles.

When a nation goes to war, it places certain demands upon its soldiers in order to save lives and protect national interest. The same is true in spiritual warfare. Strict demands must be made on all God's soldiers in order to triumph.

Ralph Winter suggests that "we must be willing to adopt a wartime lifestyle if we are to play fair with the clear intent of Scripture that the poor of this earth, the people who sit in darkness, shall see a great light."

Materialism, riches, and even the necessities of life can sometimes cause distraction. Scripture warns against misplaced priorities. Jesus said: "But seek *first* the kingdom of God and his righteousness" (Matt. 6:33, italics added).

Some preach a materialistic gospel that makes God look like a "divine errand boy" or a "big sugar daddy in the sky." Certainly there is nothing wrong with preaching that God will meet all our needs if we meet His conditions. However, some preach that there ought to be a fine car in every driveway along with any number of other luxuries. Soon the focus shifts from warfare to materialism.

Again, there is nothing wrong with having good things in life, but material possessions become wrong when they fully occupy our attention. This holds true even for the necessities of life. If Jesus were to expound on Matthew 6:25-34, He might say, "As important as food and clothing are, you must realize that the battle being waged in the heavens needs to be your first priority. Don't worry or be concerned about secondary matters. If your Father can take care of birds and flowers, which He does quite easily, then it will be a simple matter for Him to take care of your needs as well."

How often we are tempted with one of Satan's subtle deceptions. "Just take enough time to get ahead monetarily. Once you have achieved financial security, you will be able to serve God better. You won't have to worry about money." What a lie! And sadly, many Christians fall for it. Many spend their time and energy seeking riches rather than God, riches that can never secure happiness or a place in God's kingdom. If you place your confidence in money, you ignore God's promises to provide for you.

True, we need to pursue life's needs and fulfill basic obligations, but only after first seeking the kingdom of God. "But those who desire to be rich fall into temptation and a snare, and into many foolish and harmful lusts which drown men in destruction and perdition" (1 Tim. 6:9).

It isn't the riches that cause trouble; it's the inordinate desire and constant attention placed on them. Scripture doesn't say, "Where your heart is there will your treasure be also." It says, "For where your treasure is there your heart will be also" (Matt. 6:21).

4. *Conquering spiritual pride.* Most people who have been effectively used by the Lord will, no doubt, confirm that pride is no small enemy. According to Paul Billheimer:

> Very few can take honors, either from the world or from God, without becoming conceited. What servant of the Lord does not

know the subtle temptation to spiritual pride that follows even mediocre success? How often one relates an answer to prayer in such a way as to reflect credit upon oneself—and then ends up blandly saying "To God be the glory." The ego is so swollen by the fall that it is an easy prey for Satan and his demons. . . .

Who knows how much God would do for His servants if He dared. If one does not boast openly following an anointed fluency of speech, a specific answer to prayer, a miracle of faith or some other manifestation of spiritual gifts, or even graces, he is tempted to gloat secretly because of the recognition. Except for special grace on such occasions, one falls easily into Satan's trap. Because most men are so vulnerable to any small stimulus to pride, God, although He loves to do so, dares not honor many before the world by special displays of His miracle-working power in answer to prayer.[2]

It is absolutely necessary for God to deal with pride before He can use us in any meaningful way. Billheimer continues:

For until God has wrought a work of true humility and brokenness in His servants, He cannot answer some of their prayers without undue risk of producing the pride that goes before a fall. If God could trust the petitioner to keep lowly, who knows how many more answers to prayer He could readily give?[3]

Mighty power is available to the believer who prepares properly to receive it. However, God has special timing for much of what He does. Unfortunately, we often find it difficult to understand this concept, and we easily become discouraged when things do not happen as quickly as anticipated.

How do you rate on these "preparations for power"?

	Good	Need Improvement
Knowledge of God's Word	_____	_____
Resisting the sins of the flesh	_____	_____
Relinquishing the cares of this life	_____	_____
Conquering spiritual pride	_____	_____

Create a plan for improvement where needed.
_____
_____

Although we have tremendous power available, we still need God's armor to shield us from attack. The Bible speaks in specific terms concerning this armor.

Arming for Defense

Scripture commands us to be properly attired for battle. This is not an option, nor is it something that automatically happens through some kind of spiritual osmosis as a result of being a Christian. We are to conscientiously and prayerfully . . . "Put on the whole armor of God, that you may be able to stand against the wiles of the devil" (Eph. 6:11).

- *The belt of truth.* "Stand therefore, having girded your waist with truth, having put on the breastplate of righteousness" (Eph. 6:14).

Truth protects us in two ways. First, it offers *knowledge and understanding.* When we know the truth about a given situation, we can avoid error that might lead to bondage. Second, *it keeps out harmful spirits.* By learning to tell the truth, we avoid the problems that arise from lying. A lying spirit produces inferiority, fear, guilt, doubt, and a lack of confidence and trust. Everything that flows from us must convey truth. It is not just our words that are important; what people believe we have said counts as well. Some people give factual statements fully aware that they are misunderstood and then blandly say, "Well, at least I told the truth." Not so! Statements must be both stated and received correctly to fit into the realm of truth.

Truth frees us from bondage through obedience to Christ. "Then Jesus said to those Jews who believed Him, '*If you abide in My word,* you are My disciples indeed. And *you shall know the truth, and the truth shall make you free*'" (John 8:31–32, italics added). Notice that freedom from bondage is directly related to obedience to the teachings of Jesus: "*You shall know the truth,* and the truth shall make you free." When will you know the truth? When and "if you abide in My word."

The Scripture also speaks of "rightly dividing the *word of truth*" (2 Tim. 2:15, italics added) and "know[ing] the *spirit of truth*" (1 John 4:6, italics added).

Satan tells us that truth is different things to different people. He inspires the pessimistic question, "What is truth?"

There is perhaps no Scripture more vital to our total understanding of truth than John 14:6. Here we begin to realize that truth is not wrapped up in facts but in a person. To truly know the truth, one must know Jesus Christ. "I am the way, *the truth,* and the life" (John 14:6, italics added).

- *The breastplate of righteousness.* "Stand therefore, . . . having put on the breastplate of righteousness" (Eph. 6:14).

We often associate righteousness with perfection. Although there are some similarities, there really are more differences. Perfectionism frequently leads to self-righteousness. It suggests that the sufficiency of Calvary is not enough. It places attention on the individual rather than on Jesus and results in massive doses of introspection, which in turn often lead to false guilt and false condemnation.

The strength of righteousness, which is simply doing things the way God meant and said they should be done, is found only in Jesus. Scripture makes it clear that He is our righteousness and that it is only through Him that we can do things correctly. "But of him you are in Christ Jesus, who became for us wisdom from God—and righteousness and sanctification and redemption" (1 Cor. 1:30).

- *The preparation of the gospel of peace.* "Stand therefore . . . having shod your feet with the preparation of the gospel of peace" (Eph. 6:14–15).

To be prepared to spread the gospel, you must be ready for good works, always be up to date with God, and be ready to give a reason for the hope that is in you (1 Peter 3:15).

- *The shield of faith.* "Above all, taking the shield of faith with which you will be able to quench all the fiery darts of the wicked one" (Eph. 6:16).

How do you respond to the fiery darts of Satan (i.e., those thoughts that bring worry, fear, anxiety, depression, and discouragement)? Think about how you would use the shield of faith to defend yourself from each of the following attacks. Record your answers to use the next time Satan attacks you.

Selfishness:
_____

Covetousness:
_____

Pride:
_____

Doubt:
_____

Fear:
_____

Depression:
_____

Discouragement:
_____

Lust:
_____

Greed:
_____

Anger:
_____

- *Faith has surety and certainty.* "Now *faith is the substance* of things hoped for, *the evidence* of things not seen" (Heb. 11:1, italics added).
- *Faith has size.* "I say to you, if you have faith *as a mustard seed,* you will say to this mountain, 'Move from here to there,' and it will move; and nothing will be impossible for you" (Matt. 17:20, italics added).
- *Faith has measure.* "For I say . . . to everyone who is among you, not to think of himself more highly than he ought to think, but

to think soberly, as God has dealt to each one a *measure* of faith" (Rom. 12:3, italics added).

Because faith has surety, certainty, size, and measure we must assume that it is more than something found only in the mind. Therefore we conclude that:

- *Faith is not assumption.* It is not something accepted as true without proof or demonstration. Notice Paul's words to the Corinthians: "And my speech and my preaching were not with persuasive words of human wisdom, but in demonstration of the Spirit and of power" (1 Cor. 2:4).
- *Faith is not presumption.* It is not arrogant acceptance or belief without reasonable evidence.
- *Faith is not mental assent.* It is not an accumulation of facts that we believe to be true. Nor is it trying to make ourselves believe something of which we are not reasonably sure.

What then is faith? Faith can only be recognized in the deepest part of our being—our spirit. It cannot be adequately described by reason. Therefore, it is almost impossible to define, diagram, or detail. And yet it is as real as anything that we can see or touch. God does not expect us to analyze faith, only to receive and use it.

The following steps will help you gain and build faith. First, faith comes by hearing God's Word. "So then faith *cometh* by hearing, and hearing *by the word of God*" (Rom. 10:17 KJV, italics added).

Second, acting upon faith increases faith. "For therein is the righteousness of God revealed *from faith to faith:* as it is written, 'The just shall live by faith'" (Rom. 1:17 KJV, italics added).

Third, faith comes from seeking God. "Looking unto Jesus, the author and finisher of our faith" (Heb. 12:2).

Fourth, building faith requires learning to live by His faith. "I have been crucified with Christ; it is no longer I who live, but Christ lives in me; and the life which I now live in the flesh I live *by faith in* the Son of God, who loved me and gave Himself for me" (Gal. 2:20, italics added).

Create a plan for increasing your faith. How can you:

Have more time to hear the Word of God?
_____
_____

Act upon your present faith to increase your faith?
_____
_____

Set aside more time to seek God?
_____
_____

Learn to live by faith?
_____
_____

- *The helmet of salvation.* "And take the helmet of salvation" (Eph. 6:17).

It is important to protect our minds from the kind of thinking that can cause bondage. This does not mean we should remain uninformed or naive about world events. Nor does it mean that we should not know what sin is all about.

What it does mean is that we have decided not to participate any longer in wrongdoing. We have decided not to be influenced and tempted toward sin. We have decided not to deliberately allow it to enter our mind.

ARM YOURSELF WITH DEFENSIVE WEAPONS

To protect the mind, we must consider what we allow into it. Keep in mind five important things to guard against as you put on the mind of Christ through the Word of God:

1. *Guard against negative thinking.* To take an opposite view of something is not always "negative" or destructive. In fact, it is good to be negative toward such things as sin and rebellion. The kind of negative thinking that damages involves bitterness, jealousy, hatred, anxiety, worry, and fear.

Individuals with such a disposition often generate a spirit of hopelessness. Their very demeanor seems to have as much corruption about it as do their words. For example, some Christians fall prey to a negative mind-set by allowing a certain gloom and doom mentality concerning prophesied end-time events to blot out the wonderful promises of God to His children. Many people are thus afraid to make plans or to hope for anything good in life because terrible things are to happen in the last days. The "fear not" of Matthew 10:31 and Luke 12:32 seems to have little effect on their thinking.

2. *Guard against criticism.* For the most part there is nothing wrong with evaluation. The manner or attitude with which something is done often determines whether it is right or wrong.

3. *Guard against anything that makes sin acceptable or fashionable.* We live in a time in which society, rather than the Word of God, sets the standards for living. Men and women consider right and wrong as relative. They believe what is wrong for one person is not necessarily wrong for another, regardless of what God has to say. Television programming, judicial decisions, and legislative actions place a stamp of approval on sin. Adultery, fornication, and homosexuality, which the Word of God condemns as sin, are viewed as acceptable lifestyles.

4. *Guard against fantasizing sin.* Daydreaming can be a wonderful way to relax as well as a way to visualize new inventions, but to allow the mind to carry such thinking into the realm of sin is wrong. Some would argue that it is not sin to "look" as long as one does

not "touch." But God's Word declares that sin is conceived in the mind. "For as he *thinks* in his heart, so is he" (Prov. 23:7, italics added). An appropriate translation of this Scripture would be: "People become what they open their minds to."

5. *Guard against anything that seeks to control your mind.* God made us with minds capable of making decisions. Anything that hinders this capacity is contrary to His will. Satan desires to make the human mind passive and submissive to his suggestions and demands without the ability to resist. Slavery develops out of this kind of relationship. God is not interested in controlling our minds. In allowing choice He creates a dynamic individual with personality and character unlike any other creature in the world.

Examine yourself in each of the areas discussed:

Yes   No

____   ____ I often think negatively.

____   ____ I often criticize others.

____   ____ I often compromise with thoughts that make sin acceptable or fashionable.

____   ____ I often fantasize sin in my mind.

I dabble in the following:

____ mysticism ____ horoscopes ____ crystal balls
____ palm reading ____ satanic games ____ fortune telling

- *The sword of the Spirit* (The Word of God). "And take the . . . sword of the Spirit, which is the word of God" (Eph. 6:17).

ARM YOURSELF WITH DEFENSIVE WEAPONS

This verse describes God's Word as a defensive weapon. Later we will see that it is also an offensive weapon, a two-edged sword. It is God's time-honored proclamation to bring knowledge of the truth. "For the word of God is living and powerful, and sharper than any two-edged sword, piercing even to the division of soul and spirit, and of joints and marrow, and is a discerner of the thoughts and intents of the heart" (Heb. 4:12).

We can ward off the enemy with Scripture. When our minds come under assault, the Word—quoted, or read—is capable of stopping the attack. We must learn to find Scripture to fit the situation and then use it boldly. With the help of the Holy Spirit, we must speak it forth, directing it specifically at the problem we face.

Here are a few examples:

If you are afraid, quote 2 Timothy 1:7.
If you are worried, read Matthew 6:25–34.
If you are in financial trouble, note Philippians 4:19.
When you sin, remember 1 John 1:9.
When you need strength, read Isaiah 40:31.
When temptation strikes, quote Romans 8:37.
When you are unhappy, consider Nehemiah 8:10.

List additional Scriptures for your special needs in the space provided.

_____
_____
_____

Paul ended his description of the armor of God with these words: "Praying always with all prayer and supplication in the Spirit, being watchful to this end with all perseverance and supplication for all the saints" (Eph. 6:18).

8 ARM YOURSELF WITH OFFENSIVE WEAPONS

Objectives: Through this strategy session, you will learn to:

- Arm yourself with offensive weapons, including the blood of the Lamb, the word of your testimony, the name of Jesus, praise, fasting, intercession, obedience, and abandonment.

Key Verses for This Study:

Behold, I give you the authority to trample on serpents and scorpions, and over all the power of the enemy, and nothing shall by any means hurt you. (Luke 10:19)

And they overcame him by the blood of the Lamb and by the word of their testimony, and they did not love their lives to the death. (Rev. 12:11)

Step Eight: Arm Yourself with Offensive Weapons

Peter and John's ministry among the newly redeemed in Samaria (Acts 8:15), and Paul's inquiry of the Ephesian believers upon his arrival (Acts 19:1–12) clearly demonstrate a basic posture in the early church. In essence it was: "We're under instructions to change the world. Once you have been rescued from it, you'll need power to become a threat to it. The world which contained you in its grasp until now will not release its hold on others without a fight. Power is the key to our victory, and prayer is the pathway to power."

—*Jack Hayford*

God has not only given us armor for defending ourselves, He has given us weapons and the ability to use them so that we may advance into enemy territory and wage warfare.

Offensive Weapons

- *The blood of the Lamb.* "And they overcame him *by the blood of the Lamb*" (Rev. 12:11, italics added).

Through sin, Adam turned over his dominion of earth to the enemy. This gave Satan a legal right to adversely affect us and bring us into bondage. Adam's disobedience left us under the lawful control of Satan, completely powerless to effect our own deliverance and totally subject to the influence of diabolical schemes. Thus, we became Satan's slaves.

But when Jesus came to earth, He was not under Satan's control because of His sinless nature. Satan was actually powerless against Him until Jesus took our sin upon Himself. At that point, a tremendous battle began in which Jesus came forth the victor. Jesus died in our place and quickly conquered death, hell, and the grave.

It's important to realize that our redemption has been secured only through the shed blood of Jesus. "In Him *we have redemption through His blood,* the forgiveness of sins, according to the riches of His grace" (Eph. 1:7, italics added).

STRATEGIC SPIRITUAL WARFARE

The power of the blood comes from God's willingness to forgive us as we accept Christ as our sacrifice for sin. The blood of Jesus is like a two-part document. We can hold up one part to God to secure legal access to His throne because Christ took our place and set us free and the other part to Satan to claim legal release from his power. "But now in Christ Jesus you who once were far off have been brought near by the blood of Christ" (Eph. 2:13).

What spiritual bondages in your life do you need to apply the "legal document" of the blood of Jesus Christ to?

_____

_____

- *The word of our testimony.* "And they overcame him . . . by the word of their testimony" (Rev. 12:11).

The word of our testimony is in part the righteous record we leave because Christ worked within us, changing us into new creations. This record greatly affects the lives of other people, giving them courage to go on. Testimony means "evidence" or "record" like that used in a court case.

A great example of an effective testimony is the life of David Brainerd. Brainerd was a missionary to the Indians in New York state during the early 1700s. He was saved at age twenty-one, ordained into the ministry at age twenty-five, and died of tuberculosis at age twenty-nine. In his short life, David Brainerd encountered and overcame tremendous difficulties. As a result, the life of this man, which was filled with much suffering and sorrow, encouraged countless people to continue serving the Lord in the midst of their own pain. Men like Payson, McCheyne, Carey, Edwards, and Wesley were moved by Brainerd's testimony. Others, many of them in full-time ministry, have found tremendous strength from the experiences recorded in his diary.

Since we overcome by the word of our own testimony, we should be prepared to give it. Outline your testimony here. Be sure it includes the following:

1. What I was before I came to Christ
2. How I was born again
3. How my life has changed
4. Related Scriptures from God's Word

_____

_____

_____

Overcoming by the word of our testimony perhaps implies commanding evil spirits to leave specific situations and refusing to be moved by their accusations.

During the ministry of Jesus, demons were removed by the spoken word. In Matthew 8:30–32, evil spirits were cast out and allowed to go into swine through one word—"Go." Jesus actually commanded them to depart by speaking directly to them. "With authority and power *He commands the unclean spirits*, and they come out" (Luke 4:36, italics added).

Christ desires to give His followers the same authority He had here on earth. "Behold, I give you the authority to trample on serpents and scorpions, and *over all the power of the enemy*, and nothing shall by any means hurt you" (Luke 10:19, italics added).

> Most assuredly, I say to you, he who believes in Me, the works that I do he will do also; *and greater works than these he will do*, because I go to My Father. (John 14:12, italics added)

God's Word is called the Sword of the Spirit. A sword is an offensive weapon that can launch an attack. Spiritually, the Sword of the Spirit is an offensive weapon that cuts into Satan's territory.

There are two different words used in Scripture for the Word of God. *Logos* refers to the total utterance of God and the complete revelation of all He wants mankind to know. It is the Bible.

The second word, *rhema*, refers to specific words of God that have special application to individual situations. Jesus used specific *rhema* Scriptures to defend against the temptations of Satan. He also used them to wage offensive spiritual warfare. "The Spirit of the LORD is upon Me, / Because He has anointed Me / To preach the gospel to the poor; / He has sent Me to heal the brokenhearted, / To proclaim liberty to the captives / And recovery of sight to the blind, / To set at liberty those who are oppressed; / To proclaim the acceptable year of the LORD" (Luke 4:18–19). When Jesus quoted this passage from the Old Testament, He was waging offensive warfare on Satan by declaring the purposes for which He had come into the world. It was a declaration of war. He had come to set captives free!

Make a list of the problems that face you. Beside each problem list a *rhema* Scripture from the Word of God that applies to that situation, as shown in the example.

Problem	Scripture Reference
Example: I am fearful over an impending decision.	"God has not given us a spirit of fear" (2 Tim. 1:7).
_____	_____
_____	_____

- *The name of Jesus.* The name of Jesus carries authority against the works of the enemy. Note the power for healing in His name. "Then Peter said, 'Silver and gold I do not have, but what I do have I give you: In the *name of Jesus Christ* of Nazareth, rise up and walk.' . . . And His name, through faith in *His name*, has made this man strong, whom you see and know" (Acts 3:6, 16, italics added).

There is also power in His name for other miracles. "And these signs will follow those who believe: In My name they will cast out demons; they will speak with new tongues; they will take up serpents; and if they drink anything deadly, it will by no means hurt them; they will lay hands on the sick, and they will recover" (Mark 16:17–18).

The name of Jesus is not a magical formula to be used to conclude a prayer in order to guarantee its answer. The name of Jesus signifies power through invested authority. When a police officer detains a person, he has the right to say, "I arrest you in the name of the law." This means: "I arrest you according to the authority invested in me by the government I represent." No magic is involved at all, just delegated authority.

Since all power, both in heaven and on earth, now belongs to Jesus (see Matt. 28:18), He can give it to those who belong to Him. We can stop demon activity "in the name of Jesus." We can actually say, "I arrest you according to the authority invested in me by Jesus Christ." But we had better be authorized to use His power or we might meet with a similar fate as the sons of Sceva in Acts 19:13–17. Study this passage and answer the following questions:

Do demons recognize a person who has been in the presence of God?

_____

Did the demons know Paul's name?

_____

Did the demons recognize the name of Jesus?

_____

Did they recognize the names of the sons of Sceva?

- *Praise.* "Now when they began to sing and to praise, the LORD set ambushes against the people of Ammon, Moab, and Mount Seir, who had come against Judah; and they were defeated" (2 Chron. 20:22).

The three tribes mentioned in this passage were set against Judah in direct opposition to God. They were men ruled by the enemy. The power of praise destroyed Satan's endeavors in them.

Although God is pleased with praise, Satan and his demons hate it because it is something Satan has wanted desperately, but has never received. Satan cannot truly be praised because praise is a response to love, and he does not love humankind. Praise esteems the virtue of another. Since there is no virtue in Satan, it is impossible to praise him. All so-called Satan worship is a counterfeit.

When Satan's demons hear us praise God from our hearts, they hate it and flee. It is quite possible that the joyous sound coming from the singers in the 2 Chronicles account drove the demons who possessed these invaders into a such a frenzy that the men actually began killing each other.

Praise also adds strength to the life of a believer. The psalmist, who loved to praise God, wrote "But I will sing of Your power; / Yes, I will sing aloud of Your mercy in the morning; / For You have been my defense / And refuge in the day of my trouble. / To You, O my Strength, *I will sing praises;* / For God is my defense, / My God of mercy" (Ps. 59:16–17, italics added).

Turn to the book of Psalms. Read several psalms aloud and then try singing some of them. Use the psalms to help you praise and worship God in your prayer time. Record the references of some of the psalms you can effectively use for this purpose.

- *Fasting.* "Then I proclaimed a fast there at the river of Ahava, that we might humble ourselves before our God, to seek from Him the right way for us and our little ones and all our possessions.... So we fasted and entreated our God for this, and He answered our prayer" (Ezra 8:21, 23).

Fasting is not intended to secure the attention of a reluctant God. It brings us to a place where we can hear Him. Fasting does not change God, it changes us. Since God responds to us on the basis of our actions, when we change, God's response to us may change. For example, when the wicked residents of Ninevah fasted, God responded and did not destroy their city.

God desires communication with the human spirit. This becomes virtually impossible if our spirit is subject to the body and soul rather than the soul and body being subject to the spirit. Fasting sets the desires of the body aside temporarily so that the spirit is unhindered in communing with God.

Here are some scriptural guidelines for fasting:

a. Fasting is a personal matter between an individual and God: Matthew 6:16–18
b. A total fast is when you do not eat or drink at all: Acts 9:9
c. A partial fast is when the diet is restricted: Daniel 10:3
d. Leaders may call a public fast and request the whole church fellowship to fast: Joel 2:15

The purposes of fasting include:

a. Humbling yourself: Psalms 35:13; 69:10
b. Repenting of sin: Joel 2:12
c. Receiving revelation: Daniel 9:2; 3:21–22
d. Loosening the bands of wickedness, lifting heavy burdens, setting the oppressed free, and breaking every bondage: Isaiah 58:6

    e. Feeding the poor, both physically and spiritually: Isaiah 58:7
    f. Being heard of God: 2 Samuel 12:16, 22; Jonah 3:5, 10

- *Intercession.* Intercessory prayer allows a believer to stand before God on behalf of someone else. When we intercede for others, we are united with God to do spiritual warfare on their behalf.

    The most unique aspect of intercession is violent praying. It radically reorients the spiritual dimension around us. It is not much used where Christians do not understand the violence of the war going on about them: "And from the days of John the Baptist until now the kingdom of heaven suffereth violence, and the violent take it by force" (Matt. 11:12 KJV).
    All Christians should intercede at times, but some have a special calling to intercession. This powerful ministry brings the intercessor before the Lord where mighty battles rage in the unseen realm.
    On a separate sheet of paper, make a list of names of people you know who need prayer. Use the pattern below to organize your list. Intercede specifically for them in your prayer time, and record the results on the chart.

Name	Problem	Scripture to Claim for This Individual	Date Praying Began	Date Answered
___	___	___	___	___
___	___	___	___	___

- *Obedience.* Spontaneous obedience out of a heart filled with love and respect makes it difficult for the enemy to bring bondage by encouraging sin. People in love with God just don't want to sin. Jesus is our example of perfect obedience. He obeyed God the Father in every area of life and ministry, including suffering the death of the cross for the sins of all.

ARM YOURSELF WITH OFFENSIVE WEAPONS

Prayerfully examine your life. Are you obeying God in finances, business, relationships, and thought? In which areas do you need prayer?

_____
_____

- *Abandonment.* ". . . they did not love their lives to the death" (Rev. 12:11).

We try desperately to hold on to the things of this life, hoping they will provide the security and peace of mind we need. Yet that very act only separates us further from the One who can fulfill our deepest needs.

As we learn to place everything we have in God's hands, we experience a sweet communion that produces a confidence enabling us to assume a powerful offensive position in confrontations with the enemy. "I will no longer talk much with you, for the ruler of this world is coming, and he has nothing in Me. But that the world may know that I love the Father, *and as the Father gave Me commandment, so I do*" (John 14:30–31, italics added).

Rate yourself on how you are using the offensive weapons described in this chapter.

	I Use This Weapon	I Do Not Use This Weapon
The blood of the Lamb	_____	_____
The word of your testimony	_____	_____
The name of Jesus	_____	_____
Praise and singing	_____	_____
Fasting	_____	_____
Intercession	_____	_____
Obedience	_____	_____
Abandonment	_____	_____

9 EMPLOY OFFENSIVE AND DEFENSIVE STRATEGIES

Objectives: Through this strategy session, you will learn to:

- Use defensive battle strategies, including putting on the whole armor of God, submitting and resisting, not giving place to the devil, recovering yourself from the devil, abstaining from fleshly lusts, shunning profane babblings, standing your ground, trying the spirits, rejecting false teachers, laying aside worldly entanglements, and putting off evil behavior.
- Use offensive battle strategies, including arming yourself with the mind of Christ, waging war against the enemy, pulling and casting down strongholds, binding and loosening, wrestling with the enemy, speaking the Word, and learning to abide.

Key Verses for This Study:

> Put on the whole armor of God, that you may be able to stand against the wiles of the devil. (Eph. 6:11)

> Therefore submit to God. Resist the devil and he will flee from you. (James 4:7)

> Be sober, be vigilant; because your adversary the devil walks about like a roaring lion, seeking whom he may devour. (1 Peter 5:8–9)

Step Nine: Employ Offensive and Defensive Strategies

Some have taken the extreme position of assigning to Satan the material universe and everything that is in the world today, not recognizing the fact that no material or physical thing is evil of itself. God created all things good. Satan has created nothing, and his present relation to the world is only as a permitted usurper who appropriates and devastates the things of God in the interest of his own ambition.

—*Lewis Sperry Chafer*

In Chapters 7 and 8 we studied offensive and defensive weapons. In this lesson we will learn the strategies of spiritual warfare for using these weapons.

Defensive warfare is waged to defend territory, to pull forces together in response to a strike by the enemy, and to build defenses in areas where the enemy might repeat attacks.

Offensive warfare is aggressive. It takes the initiative in attack. The enemy is identified, his strategy recognized, and advances are made against him. Offensive warfare gains territory rather than defending it, and it is the only type of spiritual warfare that will reach the world with the gospel of Jesus Christ.

We cannot remain in our comfortable homes and churches and practice only defensive strategies. The army of God must advance into enemy territory. We must go against the strongholds of Satan with the power of the gospel message. We must wage aggressive, offensive warfare.

Defensive Strategies of Spiritual Warfare

The Bible teaches the following defensive actions for believers to take.

- *Put on the whole armor of God.* Is the armor of God in place? If not, or you are not sure, then the strategy is to learn how to put it on. "Put on" indicates action that we must take. This does not happen automatically. The best way to begin is to prayerfully go before the Lord and ask Him to show us how to put on the six pieces of spiritual armor. "Put on the whole armor of God, that you may be able to stand against the wiles of the devil" (Eph. 6:11).

Earlier we studied this armor. Now we must inspect it. Evaluate yourself on your use of the following weapons.

The belt of truth. Jesus Christ and His Word are truth. Are you receiving and acting upon the truth of the Word of God as it is revealed to you?

_____

How are you effectively using the truth of God's Word in your life?

_____
_____

How could you expand the application of God's truths in your life?

_____
_____

The breastplate of righteousness. Jesus Christ is the basis of your righteous standing before God. If you have the breastplate of His righteousness on, it will protect your heart and emotions against attacks of the enemy that would tempt you to engage in sinful thoughts or actions. How are you using the breastplate of righteousness to cover your heart and emotions?

_____
_____

OFFENSIVE AND DEFENSIVE STRATEGIES

How do you need to use the breastplate more effectively?

___

The preparation of the gospel of peace. The peace that comes from the gospel makes us able to fight. But we must be prepared to do so.

How are you preparing yourself to be a messenger of the gospel of peace?

___
___

In what areas of life do you need to more effectively apply this defensive weapon?

___
___

The shield of faith. Faith is acting on your belief, trusting God in spite of the difficult circumstances of life. Such faith deflects the fiery darts of unbelief hurled by the enemy.

Are you effectively using your shield of faith to deflect these fiery darts of unbelief? How are you doing this?

___
___

How could you more effectively use your faith to deal with the strategy of unbelief?

___
___

The helmet of salvation. This helmet is designed to protect the mind. Salvation includes payment for the penalties of sins of the past, including our feelings of guilt and shame. We can also be saved from the power of sin in the present.

How are you effectively using the helmet of salvation to cover the guilt of past sins and the power of sin in the present?

How could you use the helmet of salvation more effectively?

The Sword of the Spirit. The Sword of the Spirit is the Word of God, which is to be used both offensively and defensively in our spiritual warfare.

How have you recently used the Sword of the Spirit to defend against enemy attacks?

How have you recently used the Sword of the Spirit to wage offensive warfare?

What steps could you take to use the Sword of the Spirit more effectively in your spiritual walk?

- *Submit and resist.* "Therefore submit to God. Resist the devil and he will flee from you" (James 4:7).

    To resist Satan, we must have an attitude of submission to God. Defeat will result if we act independently of the Lord. The humble, not the arrogant and self-confident, overcome the enemy. "Therefore

OFFENSIVE AND DEFENSIVE STRATEGIES

humble yourselves under the mighty hand of God, that He may exalt you in due time" (1 Peter 5:6).

To resist means to "stand firm against and oppose the enemy at every point." "Be sober, be vigilant; because your adversary the devil walks about like a roaring lion, seeking whom he may devour. Resist him, steadfast in the faith, knowing that the same sufferings are experienced by your brotherhood in the world" (1 Peter 5:8-9).

Our resistance to enemy forces is based on faith. Resisting in the faith means resisting on the basis of the authority of God's Word.

Both submission and resistance are necessary to make Satan flee. What areas of your life do you need to submit to God? List these and pray about them.

_____

_____

In what areas of your life do you need to resist Satan? List these and pray about them.

_____

_____

- *Do not give place to the devil.* Do not leave room for Satan to operate "... nor give place to the devil" (Eph. 4:27). Identify every element of godlessness that endeavors to creep into your life and refuse its operation. Giving place to the devil provides him a foothold where he can operate in our lives. Footholds are generally granted through such things as alcohol, drugs, pornography, immorality, witchcraft, cults, and rebellion.

List any footholds where the enemy operates in your life and pray about them.

_____

_____

Demons endeavor to gain footholds in our attitudes and words toward others that tend to strain and ruin relationships. Carefully watch your demeanor and what you say.

- *Recover yourself from the devil.* We have a responsibility to recover ourselves from Satan's snare. Simply put, we are responsible for a certain amount of personal deliverance. "And that they may come to their senses and escape the snare of the devil, having been taken captive by him to do his will" (2 Tim. 2:26).

Think about any bondage you have in your life. What can you do to recover yourself from the trap of the devil in these areas?

Bondage	Steps I Can Take to Recover from Satan's Trap
_____	_____
_____	_____

- *Abstain from fleshly lusts. Abstain* means "to deliberately refrain as often as is necessary from an evil practice." Seventeen works of the flesh, from which we need to abstain, are listed in Galatians 5:19–21.

    Beloved, I beg you as sojourners and pilgrims, abstain from fleshly lusts which war against the soul. (1 Peter 2:11)

    Abstain from every form of evil. (1 Thess. 5:22)

Take a few minutes for a personal check-up. Read the definitions of the works of the flesh, and place a check mark by those with which you struggle. Pray about these areas.

____ Adultery: Sexual intercourse between a married person and someone who is not his or her spouse

- __ Fornication: Sexual intercourse, with mutual consent, between two people not married to each other
- __ Uncleanness: Spiritual and moral sinfulness
- __ Licentiousness: Lust, sinful emotions, lewdness
- __ Idolatry: Worship of idols
- __ Sorcery: The practice of witches
- __ Hatred: Strong feelings of dislike
- __ Contentions: Disagreement and dissention
- __ Jealousies: Rivalry, a desire to copy others to equal or excel them
- __ Wrath: Violent anger, rage
- __ Selfish ambitions: Quarreling and fighting
- __ Dissentions: Stirring up discord
- __ Heresies: Beliefs contrary to God's Word
- __ Envy: Jealousy excited by the success of others
- __ Murders: Taking the life of another
- __ Drunkenness: Excessive drinking, addiction
- __ Revelries: Worldly, boisterous merrymaking or festivities

- *Shun profane babblings. Shun* means "to avoid or to turn away from." We should avoid everything related to the enemy and to sin. Idle and unnecessary words cause many problems. "But shun profane and vain babblings, for they will increase to more ungodliness" (2 Tim. 2:16).

Profane and idle babblings are evil talk and pointless chatter, including swearing, cussing, telling off-color jokes, and other types of evil communication. Do you have a problem with this in your life? What could you do to avoid this?

- *Stand your ground.* When we stand our ground, we defend that which is rightfully ours. "Therefore take up the whole armor of God, that you may be able to withstand in the evil day, and having done all, to stand. *Stand therefore,* having girded your waist with truth, having put on the breastplate of righteousness" (Eph. 6:13–14, italics added).

Has the enemy taken spiritual territory that is rightfully yours? What can you do to reclaim it?

- *Try the spirits.* We must be alert to the deceptions of the enemy. "You therefore, beloved, since you know this beforehand, beware lest you also fall from your own steadfastness, being led away with the error of the wicked" (2 Peter 3:17). "Now the Spirit expressly says that in latter times some will depart from the faith, giving heed to deceiving spirits and doctrines of demons" (1 Tim. 4:1). We can defend against deception by trying the spirits, which means "examining for discernment." Trying the spirits helps prevent deception. We must be careful to test every spirit, in the light of God's Word. "Beloved, do not believe every spirit, but test the spirits, whether they are of God; because many false prophets have gone out into the world" (1 John 4:1).

Is every teacher and preacher truly ordained by God?

- *Reject false teachers.* False, immature, and deceived teachers are not the same. We must take care not to place all of them in the same category. *False teachers* teach doctrines, both true and false, for their own gain. Not really interested in truth or in other people, their only interest is in themselves. *Immature teachers* often espouse things not totally accurate but correct them as they grow in the Lord. *Deceived* teachers believe they are doing right, but they are not.

OFFENSIVE AND DEFENSIVE STRATEGIES

"If anyone comes to you and does not bring this doctrine, do not receive him into your house nor greet him; for he who greets him shares in his evil deeds" (2 John 10-11). How can you recognize a false teacher?

_____

Do you know any false, immature, or deceived teachers? How should you respond to them?

_____

- *Lay aside worldly entanglements.* We should lay aside worldly affairs that prevent us from being good soldiers. "Therefore, lay aside all filthiness and overflow of wickedness, and receive with meekness the implanted word, which is able to save your souls" (James 1:21).

Are there some "worldly entanglements" in your life? If so, list them below and indicate how you might deal with each.

_____
_____

- *Put off evil behavior.* Study Ephesians 4:17-32. Note the defensive action believers must take in putting off evil behavior.

Rate yourself on the defensive warfare strategies discussed in this lesson.

Defensive Strategies	I Use This Strategy	I Do Not Use This Strategy
Put on the whole armor of God	_____	_____
Submit and resist	_____	_____
Do not give place to the devil	_____	_____
Recover yourself from the devil	_____	_____
Abstain from fleshly lusts	_____	_____

Defensive Strategies	I Use This Strategy	I Do Not Use This Strategy
Shun profane babblings	_____	_____
Stand your ground	_____	_____
Try the spirits	_____	_____
Reject false teachers	_____	_____
Lay aside worldly entanglements	_____	_____
Put off evil behavior	_____	_____

Offensive Strategies of Spiritual Warfare

In addition to waging defensive warfare, we are also to put on the proper attitudes and actions of a true Christian warrior and wage offensive warfare, to fight against the strongholds of the enemy—those places where he has bound the lives of men and women. "For though we walk in the flesh, we do not war according to the flesh. For the weapons of our warfare are not carnal but mighty in God for pulling down strongholds" (2 Cor. 10:3-4).

Here are some things to consider as we prepare ourselves for the Lord's use against the enemy.

- *Arm yourself with the mind of Christ.* "Therefore, since Christ suffered for us in the flesh, arm yourselves also with the same mind, for he who has suffered in the flesh has ceased from sin" (1 Peter 4:1). "Let this mind be in you which was also in Christ Jesus, who, being in the form of God, did not consider it robbery to be equal with God, but made Himself of no reputation, taking the form of a bondservant, and coming in the likeness of men. And being found in appearance as a man, He humbled Himself and became obedient to the point of death, even the death of the cross" (Phil. 2:5-8).

OFFENSIVE AND DEFENSIVE STRATEGIES

The mind of Jesus is not automatically developed in us. We must let or permit it to do so. We must take aggressive action to arm ourselves with a similar mental attitude. "And do not be conformed to this world, but be transformed by the renewing of your mind, that you may prove what is that good and acceptable and perfect will of God" (Rom. 12:2).

To be *transformed* means "to experience a complete change that will be expressed in character and conduct." Renewing and arming our minds with Christlikeness results in such transformation. "Therefore, if anyone is in Christ, he is a new creation; old things have passed away; behold, all things have become new" (2 Cor. 5:17).

Rate yourself on a scale of 1 (low) to 10 (high) in each of the following areas:

    ___ I am letting the mind of Christ be developed in me.
    ___ I am submitting to the process of transformation.
    ___ I am conforming to the world in the following areas:

    _____

    (Pray about these.)
    ___ I have problems with my thought life in the following areas:

    _____

    (Pray about these.)

- *Wage war against the enemy.* Effective warriors cannot stand on the sidelines; we must wage war against the enemy. "Fight the good fight of faith, lay hold on eternal life, to which you were also called and have confessed the good confession in the presence of many witnesses" (1 Tim. 6:12). "This charge I commit to you, . . . that . . . you may wage the good warfare" (1 Tim. 1:18). God calls us to fight intelligently and with purpose. "Therefore I run thus: not with uncertainty. Thus I fight: not as one who beats the air" (1 Cor. 9:26).

Offensive warfare takes territory. With defensive warfare, you respond. For example, if Satan attacks your children, you become concerned and start to pray for and instruct them from God's Word. But offensive strategies work on behalf of that child *before* a rebellious spirit has opportunity to develop. By praying for and with your children and training them in the ways of the Lord, you can help shield them against Satan. In what areas of your life do you need to switch from defensive to offensive strategies?

_____

_____

- *Pull and cast down strongholds.* One of the goals of offensive warfare is to pull and cast down the strongholds of the enemy. "For the weapons of our warfare are not carnal but mighty in God for pulling down strongholds, casting down arguments and every high thing that exalts itself against the knowledge of God, bringing every thought into captivity to the obedience of Christ" (2 Cor. 10:4–5).

   Pull down means "to take down by effort or force." *Cast* means "to throw or hurl." We are told to cast off the works of darkness (Rom. 13:12) and cast out demon powers (Matt. 10:8), demolishing arguments and pretensions and taking captive any thought that is contrary to the thoughts of Christ.

Strongholds of Satan are areas in our lives where the devil working through demons has established bondage. These may be bad habits, wrong attitudes, addictions, and so on. List the strongholds of the enemy in your life.

_____

_____

OFFENSIVE AND DEFENSIVE STRATEGIES

List some strongholds you have seen in others that you need to guard against.

_____

- *Bind and loosen.* We have the power to bind the forces of evil and loosen the forces of good. "And I will give you the keys of the kingdom of heaven, and whatever you bind on earth will be bound in heaven, and whatever you loose on earth will be loosed in heaven" (Matt. 16:19).

The authority to bind and loosen implies offensive rather than defensive action. Through delegation of power and authority from Jesus, we can stop (bind) and initiate (loosen) spiritual forces. For example, through prayer we can bind the spirit of iniquity working in the life of a lost loved one, and we can ask the Holy Spirit to work in that person's life to bring him or her to a saving knowledge of Jesus Christ.

Use this spiritual weapon right now. Identify and bind the forces of evil presently working against you, and loosen the spiritual forces of the Holy Spirit.

Forces of Evil to Be Bound	**Spiritual Forces to Loose**
_____	_____
_____	_____

- *Wrestle with the enemy.* One of the most powerful verses on offensive spiritual combat is "For we do not wrestle against flesh and blood, but against principalities, against powers, against the rulers of the darkness of this age, against spiritual hosts of wickedness in the heavenly places" (Eph. 6:12).

Paul's choice of the word *wrestle* is significant, for it means "to contend in struggle for power over an opponent."

- *Speak the Word.* Jesus used the Scriptures in attacking Satan. Being deputized by Him gives us the right to do the same. Use Scripture not only for comfort, but also as a weapon. For instance, when fear tries to invade your mind, quote 2 Timothy 1:7 authoritatively: "For God has not given us a spirit of fear, but of power and of love and of a sound mind."

Find and make note of verses that apply to the following common satanic attacks. Use this list the next time you are attacked.

Attack of Satan	Scripture Reference to Use
Addictions	
Anger	
Bitterness	
Discouragement and depression	
False guilt	
Fear	
Loneliness	
Lust and immoral thoughts	
Negative thinking	
Temptation	

(Note: The presence of these conditions may not always represent a satanic attack, but satanic attacks can trigger these conditions.)

- *Learn to abide.* Life has many disappointments that faith should overcome. In many cases, faith does persevere and win the battle, but in many other situations, pain and unanswered questions may remain. You may hear, "The problem is not God, it is you"; or "If you only had faith, this wouldn't be happening to you"; or "There must be some secret sin in your life." While these statements may be true, often they are not. Many things in life cannot be answered or understood until eternity. In these situations, we

OFFENSIVE AND DEFENSIVE STRATEGIES

must learn to abide, to head down life's road with God despite our questions.

Rate yourself on the offensive warfare strategies discussed in this lesson.

Offensive Strategies	I Use This Strategy	I Do Not Use This Strategy
Arm yourself with the mind of Christ		
War against the enemy		
Pull and cast down strongholds		
Bind and loosen		
Wrestle with the enemy		
Speak the Word		
Learn to abide		

ENTERING THE COMBAT ZONE

Basic training is useless until we put that learning into action. Even a mobilized army equipped with weapons cannot be effective if it stands inactive on the sidelines. We must actually enter the combat zone.

During an invasion in the natural world, an army enters the combat zone to conquer its foes and claim new territory. In this section you, too, will invade and learn to take strategic territory, resist enemy propaganda, set captives free, rescue the wounded, and deliver the demonized.

10 TAKE STRATEGIC TERRITORY

Objectives: Through this strategy session, you will learn to:

- Identify the spiritual battlefield
- Know where the battle begins
- Identify two kinds of minds
- Explain why Satan attacks the mind
- Recognize the fiery darts from the enemy
- Resist Satan's work against the mind
- Explain the results of Satan's fiery darts
- Win the battle of the mind
- Control your spiritual gates

Key Verses for This Study:

> For though we walk in the flesh, we do not war according to the flesh. For the weapons of our warfare are not carnal but mighty in God for pulling down strongholds, casting down arguments and every high thing that exalts itself against the knowledge of God, bringing every thought into captivity to the obedience of Christ. (2 Cor. 10:3–5)

> Therefore gird up the loins of your mind, be sober, and rest your hope fully upon the grace that is to be brought to you at the revelation of Jesus Christ. (1 Peter 1:13)

> Let this mind be in you which was also in Christ Jesus. (Phil. 2:5)

Step Ten: Take Strategic Territory

> Humanity is beset by a host of self-conscious evil spirit personalities called demons, who are responsible for much, if not most, of the personality difficulties, complexities, spiritual pressures, and strains and the aggravated forms of evil that characterize our modern social order. We hold that the fallen condition of mankind, the sin of the human heart alone does not explain the abnormal psychoses and the universal snarling and fouling of human relations. This constant and fiendish disruption of the human social order is explained only by the mass activity behind the scenes of a vast, well-organized host of wicked spirits under the control of their master prince. Any spiritual method or technique which ignores the presence and activity of these occult forces cannot possibly offer an adequate solution for the problems plaguing mankind.
>
> —Paul Billheimer

In this chapter we will concern ourselves with the main battlefield of spiritual warfare. We will learn where major attacks occur, what strategies Satan's demons use, and what counterstrategies we can use to defeat the enemy.

On the major battlefields of this world, we can see devastation everywhere. While similar conditions exist in spiritual warfare, they may not be as apparent because the wounds are not usually physical.

The Spiritual Battlefield

The mind is the battlefield. Spiritual warfare is waged in the mind primarily because it is the place where thinking, reasoning, understanding, and remembering take place.

Knowing Where the Battle Begins

In order to properly fight in any kind of spiritual battle, we must first understand our own makeup. Knowing how we are put together enables us to access the part of us that will fight the battles.

Many people believe that we are made up of two parts—body, the outer, tangible part and soul, the inner, intangible part. This view, however, fails to acknowledge another inner, intangible aspect of humanity called the *spirit.* If we ignore the existence of the spirit, or if we assume it equates with the soul, we will remain confused about spiritual life and warfare.

The Word of God teaches that we are made up of body, soul, and spirit. Paul introduced this theme in 1 Thessalonians 5:23 where he said, "Now may the God of peace Himself sanctify you completely; and may your whole spirit, soul, and body be preserved blameless at the coming of our Lord Jesus Christ." Genesis 2:7 also describes this trichotomy: "And the LORD God formed man of the dust [body] of the ground, and breathed into his nostrils the breath [spirit] of life; and man became a living being [soul]." Adam's soul was evidently necessary to unite his body and spirit.

Note the distinction made between soul and spirit in Hebrews 4:12: "For the word of God is living and powerful, and sharper than any two-edged sword, piercing even to the division of soul and spirit, and of joints and marrow, and is a discerner of the thoughts and intents of the heart."

The soul enables us to function in both the material and spirit realms. The soul allows the human spirit to operate in a physical body somewhat like the transmission in a car allows the engine to transfer power to the wheels.

Two Kinds of Minds

God's Word describes two kinds of minds—the carnal and the spiritual. "For to be carnally minded is death, but to be spiritually minded is life and peace. Because the carnal mind is enmity against God; for it is not subject to the law of God, nor indeed can be" (Rom. 8:6-7). The carnal mind always listens to the desires of the body while the spiritual mind is concerned about how the human spirit relates to God.

Why Satan Attacks the Mind

Satan wants to make our minds carnal in order to keep us away from God. God wants us to have spiritual minds so that we can commune with Him. Satan battles to enter the mind because it is the entrance to the spirit, where we fellowship with God. "Jesus said to him, '"You shall love the LORD your God with all your heart, with all your soul, and with all your mind." This is the first and great commandment'" (Matt. 22:37-38).

Satan also attacks the mind because the way we think affects the way we act. "For as he thinks in his heart, so is he" (Prov. 23:7).

Satan's work almost always starts with our thinking processes, where he implants his doctrines to tempt us. Once he gains control by influencing even the smallest of our thoughts, he reaches out to other areas within the body and spirit. And so we are commanded: "Therefore, having these promises, beloved, let us cleanse ourselves from all filthiness of the flesh and spirit, perfecting holiness in the fear of God" (2 Cor. 7:1). That is, let nothing flow through your soul that will harm either body or spirit.

Christ also works first in the mind, where our initial repentance takes place. The mind is vulnerable to attacks by the enemy at two times: first, when it is not being renewed in Christ through the Word of God, and second, when it is not steadfastly trusting in Him.

Fiery Darts from the Enemy

In Old Testament times, fiery darts were used as weapons. Soldiers shot flaming darts from bows over the walls of cities to destroy thatched roofs within.

In Ephesians 6:11-17 Paul described the spiritual battle with Satan, speaking of "the fiery darts of the wicked." The enemy continuously hurls such darts at us in the form of bad thoughts. We enter the battle by dealing with the thoughts that come our way. And God gives us the ability to bring "every thought into captivity" (2 Cor. 10:5).

Paul also warned that we should not be "soon shaken in mind" (2 Thess. 2:2). If you can take hold of something and shake it, you have a good deal of control over it. Satan wants to shake, agitate, disturb, topple, destroy, or exert control over our minds.

Hebrews 12:27 indicates that whatever can be shaken in your life will be shaken. What is the purpose of this shaking?

_____

What does the Bible indicate can never be shaken?

_____

Demons work to deceive the mind in order to teach their doctrines. "Now the Spirit expressly says that in latter times some will depart from the faith, giving heed to deceiving spirits and doctrines of demons" (1 Tim. 4:1).

> For such are false apostles, deceitful workers, transforming themselves into apostles of Christ. And no wonder! For Satan himself transforms himself into an angel of light. Therefore it is no great thing if his ministers also transform themselves into

ministers of righteousness, whose end will be according to their works. (2 Cor. 11:13-15)

That we should no longer be children, tossed to and fro and carried about with every wind of doctrine, by the trickery of men, in the cunning craftiness of deceitful plotting. (Eph. 4:14)

I marvel that you are turning away so soon from Him who called you in the grace of Christ, to a different gospel, which is not another; but there are some who trouble you, and want to pervert the gospel of Christ. But even if we, or an angel from heaven, preach any other gospel to you than what we have preached to you, let him be accursed. (Gal. 1:6-8)

Beware of false prophets, who come to you in sheep's clothing, but inwardly they are ravenous wolves. You will know them by their fruits. Do men gather grapes from thornbushes or figs from thistles? Even so, every good tree bears good fruit, but a bad tree bears bad fruit. (Matt. 7:15-17)

The enemy also works to blind the minds of individuals. "Whose minds the god of this age has blinded, who do not believe, lest the light of the gospel of the glory of Christ, who is the image of God, should shine on them" (2 Cor. 4:4).
But Paul exhorted us to:

Preach the word! Be ready in season and out of season. Convince, rebuke, exhort, with all longsuffering and teaching. For the time will come when they will not endure sound doctrine, but according to their own desires, because they have itching ears, they will heap up for themselves teachers; and they will turn their ears away from the truth, and be turned aside to fables. (2 Tim. 4:2-4)

The enemy uses religious demon spirits to deceive many. Believers fall prey to thoughts and ideas that appear godly and seem right. Because these thoughts and ideas seem good, we have no inclination to question them. But because they were not born in the spirit by the Holy Spirit, they do not bear fruit. Many Christians with good hearts fall for the lies of these "spirits of religion," and their efforts do little to further the kingdom of God. They are busy but not very effective people.

Many Christians want to hear from God, but we need to constantly be aware of counterfeit voices. Mature Christians exercise caution when they use the expression "God told me." They understand that whatever they have heard must be carefully confirmed through God's Word as well as by other mature Christians. Jack Hayford says, "God gives direction but man gives confirmation." God reserves the right to tell us what to do, but He allows others to confirm His will as we fellowship together, sharing our lives with each other. The Holy Spirit in others will bear witness with our spirit, either confirming or denying the input.

It is extremely important to prove every theory and to determine the source of every thought. Failure to discover the origin of what we hear or read provides the enemy with a foothold. Many become confused by dynamic revelation from demon spirits. Because it is phenomenal and powerful, they conclude it must come from God.

Satan's Work against the Mind

- *Satan works against the mind to cause us to question the authority of God.* The first temptation of humans started in the mind when Eve questioned the authority of God. Satan said to Eve, "Yea, hath God said?" That is, "Did God really say that you could not eat of the tree of knowledge of good and evil?" Questioning God and His Word can lead to doubt, unbelief, and skepticism.

Jesus closed this door of temptation by telling the enemy to get behind him. We are to do the same.

- *Satan works against the mind to cause us to use the flesh the wrong way.* We previously studied about the flesh as a source of evil. "But I see another law in my members, warring against the law of my mind, and bringing me into captivity to the law of sin which is in my members" (Rom. 7:23).

We close the door to the flesh by strengthening our spirits through the Word, prayer, and fellowship.

- *Satan works against the mind to cause us to develop wrong motives.* A motive is a reason for doing something. Motives are important because, although we look on the outward appearance (actions), God knows what is in our hearts (motives). "For the LORD does not see as man sees; for man looks at the outward appearance, but the LORD looks at the heart" (1 Sam. 16:7). "But Jesus did not commit Himself to them, because He knew all men, and had no need that anyone should testify of man, for He knew what was in man" (John 2:24–25).

Christians perform many religious activities and even enter Christian ministry for the wrong reasons on occasion. God is more concerned with motive than ministry, so we should place our concern there as well. When motives are proper, then proper ministry will follow naturally. "Shepherd the flock of God which is among you, serving as overseers, not by compulsion but willingly, not for dishonest gain but eagerly; nor as being lords over those entrusted to you, but being examples to the flock" (1 Peter 5:2–3).

We must enter ministry (no matter what form it takes—witnessing, preaching, teaching Sunday school) willingly, not because of any advantages or benefits, and not as dictators, but as examples. Satan will try to create the wrong motives for any Christian activity.

Satan will also cause wrong motives for desiring God's power. Scripture records several examples of this. Read the story of a man named Simon in Acts 8:18-23. Other examples include the disciples who wanted to call down fire from heaven (Luke 9:54); Jonah, who wanted Ninevah destroyed (Jonah 4); and David, who was wrong in numbering the people (1 Chron. 21:1).

We close the door to wrong motives by becoming servants.

- *Satan works against the mind to cause wrong attitudes.* The enemy endeavors to insert fiery darts into the mind to produce envy, jealousy, suspicion, unforgiveness, distrust, anger, hatred, intolerance, prejudice, competition, impatience, judging, criticism, covetousness, and selfishness. He also tries to cause greed, discontent, pride, vanity, egocentricity, arrogance, intellectualism, self-righteousness, and many other wrong attitudes.

We close the door to wrong attitudes by allowing the Spirit of God to help us in our daily walk.

- *Satan works against the mind to cause rebellion.* He inserts rebellious thoughts, resulting in defiance against God's authority, which we can see as self-will, stubbornness, and disobedience. "For rebellion is as the sin of witchcraft, / And stubbornness is as iniquity and idolatry" (1 Sam. 15:23).

Satan's five "I will" statements demonstrate a rebellious spirit (Isa. 14:12-14). The "I will" spirit is a way to recognize the operation of Satan in our mind.

We close the door to rebellion by submitting to God.

- *Satan works against the mind to bring hurtful accusations.* Satan is called the "accuser of our brethren" (Rev. 12:10). By way of demon spirits he sends thoughts of accusation into our minds to bring about inferiority and condemnation. His thoughts bring feelings of shame, unworthiness, and embarrassment.

We close the door to Satan's accusations by refusing to listen to him.

- *Satan works against the mind to cause sexual impurity.* In spite of Satan's temptations, we are still responsible for the way we direct our eyes. What we read and see affects the way we think. When we yield to sin, we give the enemy ground to build on. "But I say unto you that whoever looks at a woman to lust for her has already committed adultery with her in his heart" (Matt. 5:28).

We close the door to impurity by making a covenant with our eyes to look only on pure things.

- *Satan works against the mind to cause confusion.* Satan can cause indecision, confusion, and frustration when we do not resist his thoughts. We must remember that God never authors such things. "For God is not the author of confusion but of peace, as in all the churches of the saints" (1 Cor. 14:33).

We close the door to confusion by knowing and understanding the Word of God.

- *Satan works against the mind to get us to compromise ethics and morality.* The enemy tries to imbed compromising thoughts in our minds. The principles of God and Satan stand in opposition. Satan tries to get us to compromise or adjust to his spiritual standards. For example, he will tell us we need not be so holy or believe the Bible literally.

We close the door to compromise by refusing to settle for less than what is right.

- *Satan works against the mind to bring a wrong mental focus.* The enemy constantly tries to get our focus on things of the world rather than on eternal matters. "Do not love the world or the things in the world. If anyone loves the world, the love of the Father is not in him" (1 John 2:15).

  The cares of this life can actually cause the Word of God to be ineffective in our lives. Read the parable of the sower in Matthew 13, Mark 4, or Luke 8.
  Worldly cares can make us unaware of the shortness of time and the return of Jesus. "But take heed to yourselves, lest your hearts be weighed down with carousing, drunkenness, and cares of this life, and that Day come on you unexpectedly" (Luke 21:34).
  Satan will occupy our thoughts whenever possible with material rather than eternal values. Read the parable of the rich fool in Luke 12:16–21.
  Paul warned us of many who "mind earthly things" (Phil. 3:18–19) and of the love of money. "For the love of money is a root of all kinds of evil, for which some have strayed from the faith in their greediness, and pierced themselves through with many sorrows" (1 Tim. 6:10).

We close the door to a wrong outlook on life by realizing that all that is seen with natural eyes will soon pass away.

- *Satan works against the mind by dredging up old memories that need to be forgotten.* The enemy will often use memories of things seen to hold us in bondage. He will flash pictures in our minds that excite our bodies. In this way demon spirits get us to succumb to the flesh.

Tim LaHaye notes, "The old truism, 'You are what you read,' could be enlarged to, 'You are what you see.' What the eyes feast upon forms an impression on the mind, which in turn feeds the emotions. Just as drugs or alcohol influence us physically, what we see and hear affects our thoughts and emotions."

Often evil spirits reveal themselves by planting foreign thoughts that do not come from our memories. We may never have seen or experienced what we are thinking about. Rather they are brought to us firsthand by demons. Many ungodly writings and works of art have come about by such direct satanic inspiration.

We close the door to the past by confessing our sins to God, who, because of the blood of Christ, cancels all penalties.

- *Satan works against the mind by causing it to be either inactive or overactive.* A mind that thinks too much or a mind that can hardly think at all may be affected by demonic activity. At times demons endeavor to force our minds into excessive thinking; at other times they try to render us incapable of normal mental activity.

We close the door to mental damage and pain by putting on the mind of Christ and by resisting the demon involved. This may require the prayerful help of others.

- *Satan works against the mind to cause it to become impatient.* Demons often apply mental force, which is much different from the gentle constraint of the Holy Spirit when God gives direction. This powerful coercion from the enemy commands us to carry out an order without question. God's admonition to "try the spirits" (1 John 4:1) is seldom beneficial at this point because the demon involved has already suggested that any questioning is disobedience. Such demons usually apply additional pressure by instilling the thought that the matter must be accomplished in haste. If we are not aware of the enemy's devices, we scurry about at the suggestion of these evil spirits until we are spiritually, mentally, and physically worn out. Satan wants to wear out the saints.

We close the door to impatience by waiting on God.

- *Satan works against the mind to get us to withdraw from seeking God and from fellowshiping with His people.* Satan tries to isolate the believer from the rest of the body of Christ. Since believers function together in ministry, withdrawal makes the believer nonfunctional. Elijah (1 Kings 19) and Jonah (Jonah 4:5-11) both withdrew.

We close the door to isolationism by fellowshiping with God's people.

Review what you have just studied by explaining how you would deal with each of the following attacks. The first one is completed as an example for you to follow.

Questioning the authority of God

What the enemy might say: "Has God really said you cannot do this?"

How you would respond:

Following the example of Jesus, I would tell the enemy to "get behind me." I would keep the commands of God's Word regardless of my questions or feelings.

Using the flesh in the wrong way

What the enemy might say: "If it feels good, do it!"

How you would respond:

_____

Wrong motives

What the enemy might say: "This would be a great ministry position for you. People would really look up to you, and it pays quite well."

How you would respond:

_____

Wrong attitudes

What the enemy might say: "The pastor thinks he is so smart. He really is a big know-it-all."

How you would respond:

_____

Rebellion

What the enemy might say: "Don't listen to what the pastor says. You are just as anointed as he is. Go ahead and do it anyhow, even if he doesn't approve."

How you would respond:

_____

Hurtful accusations

What the enemy might say: "You are no good. Everyone knows you are a failure. You might as well give up."

How you would respond:

Sexual impurity

What the enemy might say: "You will be married in a few weeks. What's the harm?"

How you would respond:

Confusion

What the enemy might say: "You will never understand this. You just can't remember anything anymore."

How you would respond:

Compromise

What the enemy might say: "Everyone else is doing it. Why shouldn't you?"

How you would respond:

Wrong mental focus

What the enemy might say: "You have nothing to live for. Life is passing you by. You will never get ahead in life."

How you would respond:
_____

Old memories

What the enemy might say: "If God really loved you, He would not have let abuse enter your childhood."

How you would respond:
_____

An overactive or inactive mind

What the enemy might say: "You must keep wrestling with this problem. No one else will solve it for you. You cannot have rest until you resolve this issue. But you really have no way out. Maybe if you just keep going over and over it in your mind. . . ."

How you would respond:
_____

Impatience

What the enemy might say: "You have waited for God to move all these years. Maybe you should just go ahead and do it yourself!"

How you would respond:
_____

Withdrawing from God and His people

What the enemy might say: "Those people down at that church won't miss you anyhow. They don't really care about you. They only want your money."

How you would respond:

The Results of Satan's Fiery Darts

Depression, basically a problem with the human spirit, may be experienced in the soul as feelings of despair and severe mental pain, and in the body as sensations that go beyond normal fatigue.

Various forms of depression range from low spirits characterized by feelings of sadness, to severe clinical depression, which can totally debilitate a person. In the latter case, the depressed person may refuse to eat or communicate, withdraw from social contacts, or even experience delusions and hallucinations.

But not all depression is necessarily satanically induced. Many cases of depression have links to physical disorders or chemical imbalances in the body, which often respond positively to medical treatment.

Satanically inspired depression often comes as a result of a spiritual attack on the mind. Demonic thoughts improperly resisted can bring our spirits low. This is especially true in people who are not already strong in spirit and who are not aware that Satan works in this manner.

What can Satan's demons use against you to bring on depression?

Loss and the fear of loss can bring on depression. The death of a loved one or the loss of a job, self-esteem, health, friendship, or family unity—virtually any kind of loss—may cause depression. Simply being aware of our vulnerability during these crisis times allows us to defend ourselves against mental misery; it also helps us know when to give aid to others to keep them from succumbing to this inner pain. Whenever a brother or sister in Christ suffers a significant loss, we should prayerfully recognize our responsibility to provide immediate ministry.

Satan uses suppressed anger to bring on depression. Hidden or unacknowledged anger causes many deep emotional problems. Christians may suffer depression for this reason more than nonbelievers because they sometimes hold the mistaken idea that feeling angry is a sin. Yet Scripture directs us to "be angry, and do not sin" (Eph. 4:26). This indicates that if we handle anger in a proper way—not suppressing it until it forces its way out in some undesirable manner—God will approve of our healthy emotions. Note that Paul told us not to "let the sun go down while you are still angry" (Eph. 4:26 NIV). In other words, do not go to bed upset.

But many of us have trouble expressing anger without sinning in the process. Properly expressed, anger should not inspire "hatred, contentions, jealousies, outbursts of wrath" (Gal. 5:20).

Jesus demonstrated righteous anger several times. On one occasion, He overturned the table of the money changers because they had made God's house of prayer a den of robbers (Matt. 21:12-13).

Unfulfilled expectations often trigger depression. Which of us hasn't had our heart set on something we didn't get? Who hasn't had a dream that over the years fizzled? We have many hopes, desires, and plans we believe will make us happy. We sometimes strive after them so intently that when they fail to materialize we fail in spirit right along with them.

There is nothing wrong with utilizing good plans and realistic dreams. However, they should never become our source of hope. Only Christ can fill that place in the human heart. He alone is to be our hope. Then we can go ahead and desire and plan with the attitude that "if the Lord wills, we shall live and do this or that"

(James 4:15). If what we desire comes to pass we can say, "Praise the Lord." If it doesn't, we can still say "Praise the Lord," because we know God delights in giving good things to His children and that He will do so if we wait. (See Isa. 40:31; Matt. 7:11; James 1:17.)

Negativism can cause depression. An extremely dangerous attitude, negativism, can create hopelessness. It destroys faith and refuses the gift of love while enhancing rebellion and promoting deception. People have taken sides and given up allegiances because someone spoke negatively. Without grounds for their decisions, they move on emotions alone. Human nature seems to thrive on the destruction brought about by the human tongue.

One of the best gifts God gives to the redeemed is the inner caution to stay away from a negative spirit. Christ encourages us to check out all sides of a situation before making an evaluation. Never choose sides until you have all the facts, and then consider twice.

God moves in our hearts to help us see the best in everything instead of the worst. A positive attitude allows Him to fulfill Romans 8:28 in us on a regular basis. "And we know that all things work together for good to those who love God, to those who are the called according to His purpose."

Low self-esteem often leads to self-pity, which in turn leads to depression. And along the way, we often pick up negativism and suppressed anger, making the weight of depression unbearable.

The life dedicated primarily to pleasing itself has glamour and glitter but lacks substance. It screams the loudest and seems to offer the most, but it never pays off. It claims to be the real you but doesn't even come close to what God created you for. It is one of the deepest and ugliest aspects of rebellion. It is the part of you to which Satan offers deification in order to capture your attention and your loyalty.

The old nature of self has been crucified in a believer. Evil spirits, however, work to resurrect it with all of its old ways. Satan tempts us with the belief that we deserve something better in life. But we need not give in to a selfish spirit, to let it affect or inhabit our thinking. Jesus tells us that only death to self will bring about new life: "Most assuredly, I say to you, unless a grain of wheat falls into the ground and dies, it remains alone; but if it dies, it produces much grain" (John 12:24).

Let's look at three more Scriptures to meditate on to overcome depression.

> A merry heart makes a cheerful countenance, / But by sorrow of the heart the spirit is broken. (Prov. 15:13)

> All the days of the afflicted are evil, / But he who is of a merry heart has a continual feast. (Prov. 15:15)

> A merry heart does good, like medicine, / But a broken spirit dries the bones. (Prov. 17:22)

Read about Elijah's depression in 1 Kings 19:1–14 and 18–21. For background see 1 Kings 16 and 17. Answer the following questions.

Describe the events that led to Elijah's depression.
_____
_____

Describe Elijah's attitude, which brought on depression.
_____
_____

How did God deal with Elijah's depression?
_____
_____

How have your thoughts affected your attitude? How can you deal with negative thoughts more positively?
_____
_____

We do not have sufficient space to describe the tremendously adverse effects of depression. Those who suffer from this malady should not take it lightly but should research the subject and, if necessary, get professional help. There is nothing wrong with seeking Christian doctors, counselors, and pastors to help overcome the effects of depression. We fulfill the law of Christ by bearing one another's burdens (Gal. 6:2). Should you need help, make sure your counsel comes directly from the Word of God.

Discouragement

Discouragement means "to be without courage." Such is the condition when hope seems gone. It puts heavy pressure on the spirit and brings the soul into disarray.

An unknown writer describes how the devil uses discouragement to impoverish the spirit:

> It was announced that the devil was going out of business and would offer all his tools for sale to whomever would pay the price. On the night of the sale they were all attractively displayed: Malice, Hatred, Envy, Jealousy, Sensuality and Deceit among them. Each was marked with its own price.
>
> To the side lay a harmless-looking wedge-shaped tool, much worn, and priced higher than any of them. Someone asked the devil what it was. "That's Discouragement," was the reply.
>
> "Why do you have it priced so high?"
>
> "Because," replied the devil, "it is more useful to me than any of the others. I can pry open and get inside of a man's consciousness with that when I could never get near him with any of the others."

Satan often uses the circumstances of life to discourage us as he did with King David. David and his men were away from their encampment when the Amalekites invaded and captured all the women and children. Upon their return, they became tremendously discouraged. They had no idea of the welfare of their loved ones. David was distressed, but his men were so distraught that they talked of stoning him.

David could have collapsed under the weight of his discouragement, but he didn't. Instead, he began to solve his problem. First, he dealt with his spirit. Scripture says, "But David strengthened himself in the LORD his God" (1 Sam. 30:6). Next, he turned to God for direction. In the end, "David recovered all that the Amalekites had carried away" (1 Sam. 30:18). David's victory began when he refused to accept defeat in his spirit.

Let's look at two Scriptures to help overcome discouragement. The psalmist wrote: "Be of good courage, / And He shall strengthen your heart, / All you who hope in the Lord" (Ps. 31:24). And "Why are you cast down, O my soul? / And why are you disquieted within me? / Hope in God; / For I shall yet praise Him, / The help of my countenance and my God" (Ps. 43:5).

Fear

Fear comes in at least two forms. One, which we might call normal fear, is wholesome and good. It is basically a respect for something that has potential danger. There is nothing wrong with having a fear of rattlesnakes and angry dogs.

But the second kind of fear, inordinate dread, can hurt us. Ancient Greek physicians called it *phobos,* from which we get our English word *phobia.* Hundreds of phobias, many of which hinder us from reaching our full potential in life and in the service of Jesus Christ, abound.

Some common fears include failure, rejection, the unknown, death, God, Satan, demons, people, water, darkness, responsibility, financial loss, sickness, eternity, heights, loneliness, and authority.

The Bible offers several prescriptions for fear:

Do not be afraid of sudden terror, / Nor of trouble from the wicked when it comes. (Prov. 3:25)

Do not fear therefore; you are of more value than many sparrows. (Matt. 10:31)

Do not fear, little flock, for it is your Father's good pleasure to give you the kingdom. (Luke 12:32)

For God has not given us a spirit of fear, but of power and of love and of a sound mind. (2 Tim. 1:7)

The LORD is my light and my salvation; / Whom shall I fear? / The LORD is the strength of my life; / Of whom shall I be afraid? / When the wicked came against me / To eat up my flesh, / My enemies and foes, / They stumbled and fell. (Ps. 27:1-2)

Worry is a type of fear. When a Christian worries he is saying that God is not capable of taking care of that which is His.

Then He said to His disciples, "Therefore I say to you, do not worry about your life, what you will eat; nor about the body, what you will put on. Life is more than food, and the body is more than clothing." (Luke 12:22-23)

Anxiety is a form of fear:

Be anxious for nothing, but in everything by prayer and supplication, with thanksgiving, let your requests be made known to God. (Phil. 4:6)

False Guilt and Condemnation

As with fear, guilt comes in two forms. One is wholesome and good and causes an awareness of danger. It results from the knowledge of sin. Such guilt, when reckoned with, leads to confession and repentance, which leads to liberty. As long as we are sensitive to this kind of guilt, it serves as a safeguard, but it is possible to neglect it and lose its benefits.

Guilt becomes damaging when memories of past sins and failures bring us into spiritual bondage, even after they have been confessed to the Lord. Prolonged remorse interferes with our relationship to God. But Scripture makes it clear that through Christ we have forgiveness. Let's look at two verses to help overcome guilt.

> If we confess our sins, He is faithful and just to forgive us our sins and to cleanse us from all unrighteousness. (1 John 1:9)

> For I will be merciful to their unrighteousness, and their sins and their lawless deeds I will remember no more. (Heb. 8:12)

Inferiority

Psychologists refer to an unusual sense of inadequacy or persistent attitude toward self-diminishment as an inferiority complex. Such feelings are warranted in light of our sin. We have an intuitive sense that something is wrong, but we can be made right in Jesus Christ. "Therefore if anyone is in Christ, he is a new creation; old things have passed away; behold, all things have become new" (2 Cor. 5:17).

A true spirit of inadequacy and unworthiness can benefit us in serving the Lord. We need to maintain a spirit of humility; we should never see ourselves as capable of accomplishing things in and of ourselves. But in Christ we have the strength and ability necessary for doing great things.

Let's look at three more Scriptures to help overcome inferiority:

And He said to me, "My grace is sufficient for you, for My strength is made perfect in weakness." Therefore most gladly I will rather boast in my infirmities, that the power of Christ may rest upon me. (2 Cor. 12:9)

I can do all things through Christ who strengthens me. (Phil. 4:13)

Let the weak say, "I am strong." (Joel 3:10)

Pride

As with fear and guilt, we can explore two kinds of pride. Good pride develops out of patriotism, love, loyalty, dedication, and devotion. We feel pride in our children when they do good things. We also feel proud to belong to Christ.

But pride that involves a spirit of arrogance is evil. Proverbs calls expressing too high an opinion of ourselves a haughty spirit. "Pride goes before destruction, / And a haughty spirit before a fall. / Better to be of a humble spirit with the lowly, / Than to divide the spoil with the proud" (Prov. 16:18-19).

Although humility is the opposite of pride, it does not include pushing ourselves down. Some think they show humility by driving old cars, wearing ragged clothes, and living without much in this life. But humility is an attitude of the heart, not a circumstance we are in. True humility lifts others up.

These Scripture verses can help us overcome pride:

By humility and the fear of the LORD / Are riches and honor and life. (Prov. 22:4)

Likewise you younger people, submit yourselves to your elders. Yes, all of you be submissive to one another, and be clothed with humility, for "God resists the proud, / But gives grace to the humble." (1 Peter 5:5)

Hatred

Hatred, an intense dislike for someone, manifests itself in repulsion, disgust, contempt, hard feelings, holding grudges, coldness, hostility, ill will, bitterness, and prejudice. It is one of the deadliest sins known to man. Jesus actually equated it to murder. "Whoever hates his brother is a murderer, and you know that no murderer has eternal life abiding in him" (1 John 3:15).

The Bible says: "You shall not hate your brother in your heart. You shall surely rebuke your neighbor, and not bear sin because of him. You shall not take vengeance, nor bear any grudge against the children of your people, but you shall love your neighbor as yourself: I am the LORD" (Lev. 19:17–18).

The way we think can literally affect the condition of our bodies. Hatred, bitterness, negativism, and animosity create dysfunctions within the chemical and electrical systems of the human body, resulting in illness. Our hatred may lead to our own death. But many diseases can be cured simply by rearranging our thinking.

Let's look at three more Scriptures to help overcome hatred.

And be kind to one another, tenderhearted, forgiving one another, just as God in Christ also forgave you. (Eph. 4:32)

Do not withhold good from those to whom it is due, / When it is in the power of your hand to do so. (Prov. 3:27)

> The merciful man does good for his own soul, / But he who is cruel troubles his own flesh. (Prov. 11:17)

Think about the results of Satan's fiery darts, which you studied in this section. How can you combat them?

Depression:
_____
_____

Discouragement:
_____
_____

Fear:
_____
_____

False guilt and condemnation:
_____
_____

Inferiority:
_____
_____

Pride:
_____
_____

Hatred:
_____

Winning the Battle of the Mind

What a huge arsenal of fiery darts Satan has aimed at our minds! But God has provided spiritual strategies to overcome Satan's attacks.

Let the Holy Spirit Search Your Heart

Ask God to search your heart and reveal any wrong attitudes, motives, or thoughts that the enemy has planted. "Search me, O God, and know my heart; / Try me, and know my anxieties; / And see if there is any wicked way in me, / And lead me in the way everlasting" (Ps. 139:23–24). As He reveals things to you, act upon the revelation.

Use Your Spiritual Armor

Especially notice these three pieces of spiritual armor that can defend you from attacks. Wear the first, the helmet of salvation, on your head to protect your mind. Keep the second, the Word of God, which is the Sword of the Spirit, with you at all times. Use the third, the shield of faith, to fend off the enemy's fiery darts.

Claim a Sound Mind as God's Will for Your Life

To eliminate tormenting thoughts, claim the peace you rightfully deserve. "And the peace of God, which surpasses all understanding, will guard your hearts and minds through Christ Jesus" (Phil. 4:7). To do so, pray this prayer:

Dear God, I claim your peace, which passes my own human understanding, to guard my heart and every thought of my mind. I claim a sound mind as your will for me. Cover me with your peace. Amen.

Let This Mind Be in You

Paul wrote under the inspiration of the Holy Spirit: "Let this mind be in you which was also in Christ Jesus" (Phil. 2:5).

Prepare Your Mind for Action

Peter told us to strengthen our minds for action. "Therefore gird up the loins of your mind, be sober, and rest your hope fully upon the grace that is to be brought to you at the revelation of Jesus Christ" (1 Peter 1:13).

Think on These Things

One way to strengthen your mind is to think only about right things. Paul said: "Finally, brethren, whatever things are true, whatever things are noble, whatever things are just, whatever things are pure, whatever things are lovely, whatever things are of good report, if there is any virtue and if there is anything praiseworthy—meditate on these things" (Phil. 4:8).

Here are positive mental qualities you should develop. How do you measure up?

___ A ready mind: 2 Corinthians 8:19
___ A pure mind: 2 Peter 3:1
___ A stayed mind: Isaiah 26:3
___ A renewed mind: Ephesians 4:23
___ A humble mind: Colossians 3:12
___ A sober mind: Titus 2:6
___ A sound mind: 2 Timothy 1:7
___ A mind of love: Matthew 22:37
___ A serving mind: Romans 7:25
___ A fully persuaded mind: Romans 14:5
___ A fervent mind: 2 Corinthians 7:7 (KJV)
___ A willing mind: 2 Corinthians 8:12

Renew Your Mind

"And do not be conformed to this world, but be transformed by the renewing of your mind, that you may prove what is that good and acceptable and perfect will of God" (Rom. 12:2). Renew your mind through prayer and meditation on God's Word.

Encourage Yourself in the Lord

Remember that David encouraged himself in the Lord when everything seemed to be going against him. "Now David was greatly distressed, for the people spoke of stoning him, because the soul of all the people was grieved, every man for his sons and his daughters. But David strengthened himself in the LORD his God" (1 Sam. 30:6).

You must take action and encourage yourself in God. Do not wait for others to do it. Do it yourself! This is God's strategy for attacks of depression and discouragement.

Recognize the Source of Confusion

Confusion does not come from God. "For God is not the author of confusion but of peace, as in all the churches of the saints" (1 Cor. 14:33). Refuse to accept the spirit of confusion in your mind.

Keep Your Mind Steadfast on God

"You will keep him in perfect peace, / Whose mind is stayed on You, / Because he trusts in You" (Isa. 26:3). This is a great promise! If you keep your mind centered on God, you can have peace in spite of the enemy's attacks.

Rate yourself on your use of spiritual strategies for overcoming the attacks of Satan on the mind.

Strategy	I Use This Strategy	I Do Not Use This Strategy
Let the Holy Spirit search your heart		
Use your spiritual armor		
Claim a sound mind as God's will for your life		
Let this mind be in you		
Prepare your mind for action		
Think on these things		
Renew your mind		
Encourage yourself in the Lord		
Recognize the source of confusion		
Keep your mind steadfast on God		

Controlling the Gates

In Old Testament times cities were surrounded by walls for defense against enemy forces. The walls had gates, and guards controlled these entrances. Whoever controlled the gates of the city controlled the city.

A similar situation exists in controlling our minds. Our five senses make up the "gates" to our innermost being. It is vitally important that we not allow anything to enter us that has the ability to destroy from within. Using drugs and alcohol can result in mental and physical addiction, which can lead to depression, suicidal thoughts, violence, and other bizarre behavior. Pornography, certain kinds of music, witchcraft, cultic activity, mind control teaching, and traumatic experiences may also become entrance points for demons. These things are dangerous because they reduce our ability to adequately control our thought life. For more detail see "How Demons Gain Access" in Chapter 12.

11 RESIST ENEMY PROPAGANDA

Objectives: Through this strategy session, you will learn to:

- Recognize Satan's method
- Resist Satan's appeals and promises
- Reject Satan's lies and accusations
- Identify other things Satan causes men to say

Key Verses for This Study:

> Lest Satan should take advantage of us; for we are not ignorant of his devices. (2 Cor. 2:11)

> Be sober, be vigilant; because your adversary the devil walks about like a roaring lion, seeking whom he may devour. Resist him, steadfast in the faith, knowing that the same sufferings are experienced by your brotherhood in the world. (1 Peter 5:8–9)

Step Eleven: Resist Enemy Propaganda

Satan is a liar and a deceiver. He is a great imitator. As we have seen as far back as the Garden of Eden, Satan's purpose was not to make Eve as ungodly as possible, but to make her as godlike as possible without God. Satan's plan has always been to imitate God. The Scripture says, "Satan himself masquerades as an angel of light." It is not surprising, then, if his servants masquerade as servants of righteousness. Their end will be what their actions deserve."

—*Billy Graham*

Which of the following do you believe to be true?

    ___ Satan's goal is to destroy the human race.
    ___ Deception is Satan's primary tool.
    ___ Satan has a lot of creative ability.
    ___ One of the basic tenets of many false religions is the promise of deification.
    ___ Horoscopes, tarot cards, and crystal balls are basically harmless games.
    ___ Satan plants his doctrines in a person's mind.

(Return to this section and reevaluate your answers when you have completed this strategy session.)

Satan wants us to hear what he has to say. He endeavors to communicate false information in such a way that it will cause humanity to self-destruct. His goal is the destruction of our race. If we are to survive his attacks we must understand his schemes and discern his ways. As good Christian soldiers, we must learn to resist enemy propaganda.

Whenever we refer to Satan, keep in mind that many demons do his work. It is all too easy to believe that Satan is omnipresent like God when, in fact, he is only in one place at one time.

Satan's Method

Deception is the enemy's primary tool. Through falsehood and lies he tries to manipulate the human race. "He was a murderer from the beginning, and does not stand in the truth, because there is no truth in him. When he speaks a lie, he speaks from his own resources, for he is a liar and the father of it" (John 8:44).

Of the five "I will" goals of Satan recorded in Isaiah 14, one was to "be like" God. His deceptive practices include counterfeiting and imitating God's actions. He has no real creative ability in him. Even his ranking of demons imitates the organization of the angelic host. He uses a system of blood sacrifice similar to that found in covenant relationship with God. He desires adoration similar to that given to God. The only original thing that can be attributed to him is rebellion.

Satan's Appeals and Promises

Deception—"You can become a god." The enemy first appealed to Eve with the promise of godhood. She could be "like" God. All she had to do was disobey Him and eat the forbidden fruit.

The king of Tyre also fell for the lie (Ezek. 28:1-19). He proclaimed, "I am a god; / I sit in the seat of gods, / In the midst of the seas." In his deception, the king allowed the enemy to control him. At one point when God spoke to him, it appears He actually spoke to the enemy residing in him.

King Herod was likewise trapped. During one of his public speeches, the people exclaimed, "The voice of a god, and not of a man!" (Acts 12:22). This pleased Herod immensely. Instead of giving the praise to God, he allowed the people to exalt him. "Then immediately an angel of the Lord struck him, because he did not give glory to God. And he was eaten by worms and died" (Acts 12:23).

Josephus writes, "He fell into deepest sorrow . . . and he died after five days of illness."

Even today this doctrine of godhood is taught by demons. Hinduism, Mormonism, Jehovah's Witnesses, and many other cults promise deification to their followers.

God's Word says, "yet for us there is one God" (1 Cor. 8:6). We become like God only when we allow Christlike characteristics to develop in us.

Deception—"You can know the future." God wants us to trust our future to Him. Satan works at destroying God's guidance by enticing people to dabble in predicting the future. Ouija boards, crystal balls, tarot cards, horoscopes, and palm reading are a few of the tools the enemy uses to distract us from God. Although many believe these things cannot cause harm, they carry the power of demon spirits within them. They are not harmless games.

Concerning the future, God's Word says, "My times are in Your hand" (Ps. 31:15).

Deception—"You have been here before and will be here again." The doctrine of reincarnation is basically a sub-doctrine of "You can become a god." It teaches that the state of perfection required of a god takes such a long time to achieve that one may have to live many times in many different forms. The feeling that we have been here before (déjà vu) may at times have its roots in satanic suggestion.

God's Word says, "And as it is appointed for men to die once, but after this the judgment" (Heb. 9:27).

Deception—"Your eternal destiny is already determined and there is nothing you can do about it." Demons actually teach that we were born with our eternal destination pre-determined. "Some were created for heaven, others were created for hell," the demon then whispers. "You are one of the ones created for hell."

God's Word says, "[God] is longsuffering toward us, not willing that any should perish but that all should come to repentance" (2 Peter 3:9).

Have you fallen for any of Satan's deceptions? Check any that apply.

___ "You can become a god."
___ "You can know the future."
___ "You have been here before and will be here again."
___ "Your eternal destiny is already determined and there is nothing you can do about it."

Pray about any items you have checked.

Satan's Lies and Accusations

What Satan says: "You've got to clean up your life before you can come to God."
What God says: "Come now, and let us reason together," / Says the LORD. / "Though your sins are like scarlet, / They shall be as white as snow; / Though they are red like crimson, / They shall be as wool" (Isa. 1:18).
What Satan says: "Everyone is a child of God."
What God says: "He who is not with Me is against Me" (Matt. 12:30).
What Satan says: "God is too good to send anyone to hell."
What God says: "Not everyone who says to Me, 'Lord, Lord,' shall enter the kingdom of heaven, but he who does the will of My Father in heaven" (Matt. 7:21).
What Satan says: "All God expects you to do is lead a good life and do the best you can."
What God says: "Most assuredly, I say to you, unless one is born again, he cannot see the kingdom of God" (John 3:3).
What Satan says: "You have failed so many times. He won't take you back."

What the Bible says: "If we confess our sins, He is faithful and just to forgive us our sins and to cleanse us from all unrighteousness" (1 John 1:9).

What Satan says: "You will have to give up too much in order to be saved."

What God says: "And everyone who has left houses or brothers or sisters or father or mother or wife or children or lands, for My name's sake, shall receive a hundredfold, and inherit everlasting life" (Matt. 19:29).

What Satan says: "It is too hard to serve God."

What God says: "Come to Me, all you who labor and are heavy laden, and I will give you rest. Take My yoke upon you and learn from Me, for I am gentle and lowly in heart, and you will find rest for your souls. *For My yoke is easy and My burden is light*" (Matt. 11:28–30, italics added).

What Satan says: "Jesus is not the only way to heaven."

What God says about Jesus: "Nor is there salvation in any other, for there is no other name under heaven given among men by which we must be saved" (Acts 4:12).

What Satan says: "There are too many ways to interpret the Bible."

What the Bible says: "Knowing this first, that no prophecy of Scripture is of any private interpretation, for prophecy never came by the will of man, but holy men of God spoke as they were moved by the Holy Spirit" (2 Peter 1:20–21).

What Satan says: "You deserve to go to heaven because you've done the best you could."

What God says: "There is none who does good, no, not one" (Rom. 3:12).

What Satan says: "You are too weak to serve the Lord."

What God says: "My grace is sufficient for you, for My strength is made perfect in weakness" (2 Cor. 12:9).

What Satan says: "You need not worry about eternity just yet. You can do it later."

What God says: "Behold, now is the accepted time; behold, now is the day of salvation" (2 Cor. 6:2 KJV).

Have you believed any of these lies of Satan? Check the lies Satan has used against you.

- ___ "You've got to clean up your life before you can come to God."
- ___ "Everyone is a child of God."
- ___ "God is too good to send anyone to hell."
- ___ "All God expects you to do is lead a good life and do the best you can."
- ___ "You have failed so many times. He won't take you back."
- ___ "You will have to give up too much in order to be saved."
- ___ "It is too hard to serve God."
- ___ "Jesus is not the only way to heaven."
- ___ "There are many ways to interpret the Bible."
- ___ "You deserve to go to heaven because you've done the best you could."
- ___ "You are too weak to serve the Lord."
- ___ "You need not worry about eternity just yet. You can do it later."

Pray about the items you checked.

Other Things Satan Causes People to Say

There are many other things Satan causes people to say. Have you ever made any of these statements?

- ___ "Christianity may be good for some, but it is not for everyone."

___ "If God is a loving God, why does He send people to hell?"
___ "Churches have too many hypocrites."
___ "The Bible is so complicated that I can't understand it, so why bother?"
___ "You have committed the unpardonable sin. There is no hope for you."
___ "There are too many religions. How can you know who's right?"
___ "Jesus is not God."
___ "It is not necessary to think very much about eternity."
___ "As long as you are sincere, that is all that matters."
___ "I believe in God." (Belief is not enough. Even demons "believe" in God.)
___ "I believe when we die that's it."
___ "I'm as good as anybody."
___ "I'm not appreciated."
___ "I deserve better."
___ "I do not deserve to be treated this way."
___ "I'm going to get cancer."
___ "My loved ones will never be saved."
___ "Nobody cares about me."
___ "I'm not going to make it."
___ "Who cares?"
___ "Why doesn't God do something?"
___ "Where was God when I needed Him?"
___ "Why did God take that from me?"
___ "I'm no good."
___ "It's hopeless."

Pray about the items you checked.

12 SET THE CAPTIVES FREE

Objectives: Through this strategy session, you will learn to:

- Identify cities and territories taken captive by the enemy
- Identify individuals taken captive by the enemy
- Recognize demon spirits
- Explain how demons gain access
- Escape the dangers of the occult
- Guard against transference of spirits

Key Verses for This Study:

In humility correcting those who are in opposition, if God perhaps will grant them repentance, so that they may know the truth, and that they may come to their senses and escape the snare of the devil, having been taken captive by him to do his will. (2 Tim. 2:25–26)

Now the Spirit expressly says that in latter times some will depart from the faith, giving heed to deceiving spirits and doctrines of demons. (1 Tim. 4:1)

Step Twelve: Set the Captives Free

Doubt about the existence of a malign focus of evil is to be found, by and large, only in Christian lands. It is only where

the victory of Christ is so well known, only where the defeat of the devil is so celebrated, that doubts are expressed. If he exists, it must please him mightily to have his existence denied by the only people who know his inherent weakness, and are aware of the fact of Christ on Calvary that spelt his doom. Were he better known he would be more hated, more resisted, more defeated in the lives of Christians. So it suits him admirably for them to slumber in the bland assurance that he does not exist.
—*Michael Green*

Satan has a vast network of demon spirits working diligently to espouse doctrines that keep us from finding fulfillment in our Creator. Ranks of evil spirits control geographical areas of our world, working within those areas to control specific individuals.

Cities and Territories Taken Captive by the Enemy

The Bible tells of a demon spirit who controlled Persia (today called Iran). In the Old Testament when Daniel set about to seek the Lord, his prayer was heard in heaven and immediately God sent an answer by way of an angel. To get to Daniel, the angel had to pass through the land of Persia. As he did, the prince of Persia, a powerful demon, stopped him. The archangel Michael had to help the angel fight against this demonic force. Together they prevailed over him. The angel proclaimed to Daniel:

> Do not fear, Daniel, for from the first day that you set your heart to understand, and to humble yourself before your God, your words were heard; and I have come because of your words. But the prince of the kingdom of Persia withstood me twenty-one days; and behold, Michael, one of the chief princes, came

to help me, for I had been left alone there with the kings of Persia. (Dan. 10:12–13)

From this passage, it appears that demonic forces rule specific geographic areas. It is possible such forces still reign over other territories of our world. It may be possible to identify the ruling spirit of an area by studying its history. Certain patterns of demon activity can be observed in historical records. For example, in the records of the early history of one small California town, we find that in a specific area, "opium dens" and "criminal activity" were prevalent. Now, 100 years later, that town has grown into a city, and the same geographic area of that city still has a major drug problem. To study the history of your area to determine the ruling spirits, you may want to do the following:

- Visit the public library and review books that recount the history of the city
- Visit the local newspaper office and review its files
- Talk with elderly residents of the area
- Observe what spirits now operate and see if you can trace these in the history of your town

Individuals Taken Captive by the Enemy

Among the demons there appear to be high ranking officials, such as lieutenants and generals. Then there are the troops, who directly affect individuals.

Demon control is perhaps one of the greatest areas of misunderstanding and misinformation within the church. Few have taken the time or energy to adequately research this realm in order to speak knowledgeably on it. For whatever reason, there is a great deal of ignorance about demon possession.

A basic Greek word for this kind of demon activity is *daimonizomai*, which means "to be vexed with or possessed with" a demon. But when the word is translated "possessed" we somehow get the idea that the person involved *belongs to* a demon or demons. This is not the case. The word *daimonizomai* would carry a much clearer meaning if we translated it as "overwhelming demonic influence" rather than "demon possession."

C. Fred Dickason suggests, "Demons do not possess or own anything. God owns them. They are His creatures and He is their judge. If they inhabit a person, they have only squatters' rights. They violate God's laws of the sanctity of the person and his body" (1 Cor. 6:13).

That we can be affected by demon spirits is evident from Scripture. Study the following verses in the book of Matthew— 4:24; 8:16, 28-34; 9:32-34; 10:1, 8; 12:22, 43-45; 15:22-28; 17:14-21.

When demons enter a person's spirit their strong influence controls that person. If Christ lives there, demon possession isn't possible. Unfortunately, some influence still is! Demons work against Christians through the soul, and they are capable of doing so even if Christ has entered us. That is why we must constantly resist the enemy.

Since the Spirit of Christ never operates by force, we are responsible for what takes place in the realm of the soul. We must choose to submit to the lordship of Jesus Christ and to actively wage war against the devil. We must choose to deny sin and obey God's Word. In doing these things, we combat the work of the enemy against our souls.

Many Christians need deliverance from the influence of demons. In certain cases, the influence is so strong that some believers appear to be possessed. They have allowed the enemy to work in their souls. Although Christ still lives in their spirits, demons working through their souls do to them many of the things they do to unbelievers.

This is why it is so important to recognize and resist the enemy. When demons try to work in our minds, we do not need to worry about semantics (possession, oppression, influence, etc.); we need simply to resist them. When they try to move our emotions in order to make us psychological wrecks, we must resist. When we are tempted to allow hostility, resentment, or animosity to govern, we must continue to resist. In severe cases, some Christians may find it necessary for other believers to help them bind and break the power of the enemy through intercessory prayer.

Recognizing Demon Spirits

How can we recognize the presence of demons? The following list represents certain kinds of manifestations of those who are demonized. Note, however, that the presence of these kinds of behaviors *does not* always mean a demon is at work.

- Violent, uncontrolled behavior usually accompanied by incredible physical strength
- Excessive blasphemy
- Immediate and abrupt behavior change when the name of Jesus is mentioned
- Inability to say the name of Jesus (while the demon may say the name of Jesus, it usually tries to prevent the person involved from doing so)
- Inability to control the desire for pornography, adultery, fornication, masturbation, and homosexuality
- Strong compulsions toward suicide, murder, stealing, lying, and other forms of known sin
- A driving force toward hatred, jealousy, backbiting, envy, pride, bitterness, negativism, and criticism

- Extreme attitudes of bitterness, criticism, negativism, contempt for authority, rejection, and unforgiveness
- Sickness that does not yield to treatment

Recognition of demonic presence may come through:

- The gift of discernment imparted by the Holy Spirit
- The witness of the Holy Spirit (often confirmed by other Christians)
- A sensation—smell, taste, feeling

When Christians manifest the presence of demons, some may be shocked at what they witness but fail to do anything against the demons because of a theology that refuses to believe what they see.

Consider Matthew 12:22-28 and 43-45 where Jesus discusses the reality of spirits that inhabit and affect people. In view of these and other Scriptures, it is impossible for us, as conscientious, thinking Christians, to say we believe in the Bible and yet deny the reality of demons and their work.

How Demons Gain Access

The following partial list describes entry points the enemy uses to subdue people. Place a check mark by any that apply to you.

___ Use of mind-altering substances such as drugs and alcohol. These substances reduce our ability to resist demons and therefore grant them increasing influence and access.

___ Involvement in mind-control teaching. Teachings that encourage passivity (blanking out the mind) or unquestioned devotion to an individual provide entrance points for demon activity.

___ Participation in the occult. This allows the enemy major control. Ouija Boards, tarot cards, crystal balls, palm reading, and horoscopes provide open doors for enemy activity (see next section).

___ Environmental influence. Influence can be gained when we visit places where demon activity abounds (i.e., rock concerts, bars, certain kinds of parties, and any other place where sinful activity is practiced).

___ Family influence. Certain kinds of demons appear to affect some families for generations (see "Transference of Spirits").

___ Fear. This emotion seems to be an open door for demons in some people.

___ Sinful habits. To practice sin, especially known sin, grants enemy influence.

___ Defiance and rebellion. Demon activity often abounds wherever these attitudes exist.

___ Emotional violation. Severe hatred, intimidation, rejection, and so on, can attract demons.

___ Physical violation. Rape, incest, molestation, violence, sexual abuse, or other traumatic situations sometimes provide an entrance point as well.

If you checked any of the items above, you may be disturbed and wondering whether demons are affecting your actions. Whether or not, the first step in either case is not to fear. Rather, begin by examining any inappropriate or out of character behavior and deal with that manifestation.

By turning to Jesus and resisting the enemy, many if not all problems will cease. If these steps do not bring relief, get help.

Certain people within the body of Christ have been given special abilities to break the chains the enemy has over demonized individuals. Seek them out and ask for their intervention on your behalf.

(A note of caution: there are some who because of their experiences in the demonic realm assume a self-styled deliverance ministry without really being called of God. This is dangerous for them and the people to whom they endeavor to minister. A little bit of knowledge can do a lot of damage. Only those directed of the Lord to do so should attempt to practice deliverance.)

Review the access points for demonic activity. Pray specifically about those that you checked, binding the powers of Satan and repenting where necessary.

Dangers of the Occult

Many types of occultic practices may fit under the general categories of divination, spiritualism, or witchcraft.

Hydromancy: Water divining

Prognostication: Predicting or foretelling the future by means of signs and omens

Astrology: Consulting stars, horoscopes

Necromancy: Consulting the spirits of the dead

Seances: Anything depending on a spirit-guided medium

Any activities to gain "supernatural knowledge" where you and the God of the Bible are not in control: Including fortune-telling, palm reading, crystal-ball gazing, automatic writing or speaking, casting spells, placing curses, gaining "psychic blasts," levitating objects, engaging in telepathy, using ESP, handling a Ouija board, consulting crystals, reading tarot cards, and patterning bones

The practice of curanderos: Such as psychic surgery, demonic-inspired "cures" through folk medicine and superstition, magic, sorcery

Transference of Spirits

One of the most powerful and influential strategies used by the enemy is transference of spirits. Recognition of this strategy will answer many questions concerning the negative changes sometimes seen in people. *Transference of spirits* refers to someone assuming the character, mannerisms, attitudes, and motives of another. The actions of each person exhibit a certain "spirit," for example, a gentle spirit, a boisterous spirit, or a rebellious spirit. That spirit can be influenced by the spiritual forces of good or evil, and can be transferred to others on a personal or group basis.

The Importance of the Spirit

Before we study biblical examples of transference of spirits, it is necessary to understand our own spirit and why it is an important target of Satan's attack.

- God created our spirit. "Thus says the LORD, who stretches out the heavens, lays the foundation of the earth, and forms the spirit of man within him" (Zech. 12:1).

- It is the spirit that gives life. "For as the body without the spirit is dead, so faith without works is dead also" (James 2:26).
- At death, the spirit returns to God. "Then the dust will return to the earth as it was, / And the spirit will return to God who gave it" (Eccl. 12:7).
- God is Lord of our spirit. "Let the LORD, the God of the spirits of all flesh, set a man over the congregation" (Num. 27:16).
- God weighs or judges our spirit. "All the ways of a man are pure in his own eyes, / But the LORD weighs the spirits" (Prov. 16:2).
- God desires to put His Spirit (the Holy Spirit) within us so we will be able to live for Him. "I will put My Spirit within you and cause you to walk in My statutes, and you will keep My judgments and do them" (Ezek. 36:27).
- God wants to preserve our spirit in holiness until the return of Jesus Christ. "Now may the God of peace Himself sanctify you completely; and may your whole spirit, soul, and body be preserved blameless at the coming of our Lord Jesus Christ. He who calls you is faithful, who also will do it" (1 Thess. 5:23–24).
- God speaks to us in our spirit. "The Spirit Himself bears witness with our spirit that we are children of God" (Rom. 8:16).
- The human spirit is the innermost part of us. "The spirit of a man is the lamp of the LORD, / Searching all the inner depths of his heart" (Prov. 20:27).
- God acknowledges a person with a humble spirit. "But on this one will I look: / On him who is poor and of a contrite spirit, / And who trembles at My word" (Isa. 66:2).
- God lives with a person who has a humble spirit. "For thus says the High and Lofty One / Who inhabits eternity, whose name is Holy: 'I dwell in the high and holy place, / With him who has a contrite and humble spirit, / To revive the spirit of the humble, / And to revive the heart of the contrite ones'" (Isa. 57:15).
- The tongue is a powerful force and can endanger the spirit of other people. "A wholesome tongue is a tree of life, / But perverseness in it breaks the spirit" (Prov. 15:4).

Is Transference of Spirits Scriptural?

The powerful anointing of God upon Moses was transferred from him to other elders.

> So the LORD said to Moses: "Gather to Me seventy men of the elders of Israel, whom you know to be the elders of the people and officers over them; bring them to the tabernacle of meeting, that they may stand there with you. Then I will come down and talk with you there. *I will take of the Spirit that is upon you and will put the same upon them.*" (Num. 11:16-17, italics added)

Transference of an Evil Spirit

Moses sent twelve men to spy out the land God promised to Israel. Read the account in Numbers 13:17-14:39. Ten of these spies returned with a negative report. They told of great walled cities and a powerful enemy within the land. They transferred a spirit of fear and unbelief to the rest of God's people. "But the men who had gone up with him said, 'We are not able to go up against the people, for they are stronger than we. . . . There we saw the giants . . . and we were like grasshoppers in our own sight, and so we were in their sight'" (Num. 13:31, 33).

This report caused Israel to fail to obey the command of God. Subsequently, many did not see the promised land. But two of the spies had a different spirit.

> And Joshua the son of Nun and Caleb the son of Jephunneh, who were among those who had spied out the land, tore their clothes; and they spoke to all the congregation of the children of Israel, saying: "The land we passed through to spy out is an exceedingly good land. If the LORD delights in us, then He will

bring us into this land and give it to us, 'a land which flows with milk and honey.'" (Num. 14:6–8)

But *My servant Caleb, because he has a different spirit in him* and has followed Me fully, I will bring into the land where he went, and his descendants shall inherit it. (Num. 14:24, italics added)

Two different spirits were seeking to control the people. One was the spirit of unbelief, the other the spirit of belief. "Then Caleb quieted the people before Moses, and said, 'Let us go up at once and take possession, for we are well able to overcome it'" (Num. 13:30). But look how the negative spirit of the ten spies affected the people.

So all the congregation lifted up their voices and cried, and the people wept that night. And all the children of Israel complained against Moses and Aaron, and the whole congregation said to them, "If only we had died in the land of Egypt! Or if only we had died in this wilderness! Why has the Lord brought us to this land to fall by the sword, that our wives and children should become victims? Would it not be better for us to return to Egypt?" So they said to one another, "Let us select a leader and return to Egypt." (Num. 14:1–4)

These were the spirits of despair, murmuring, and rebellion transferred among God's people. God's people were not kept out of the promised land because of an inferior army but because of a wrong spirit.

Why were the people affected by the evil spirit instead of the good? Our sin nature tends to immediately accept and believe an evil report, and we tend to follow the crowd. If Israel had accepted the positive report, they would have had to expose themselves to great danger. Our human nature always wants to take the easy way out.

Transference of spirits accounts for many of the spiritual battles fought by believers today. It explains some behavior changes, especially those where people abruptly move from positive to very negative attitudes. It may explain why two children raised in the same home with the same training can turn out so differently. It is often the reason behind divisions in homes, friendships, and church fellowships. When we maintain close association with or come under the influence of a person with a spirit more powerful than ours, we are open to the transference of that person's spirit to ours.

Preventing Transference of an Evil Spirit

God has given us spiritual counterstrategies to prevent the transference of an evil spirit.

- Control your own spirit.

    Therefore take heed to your spirit, / That you do not deal treacherously. (Mal. 2:16)

    Whoever has no rule over his own spirit / Is like a city broken down, without walls. (Prov. 25:28)

    He who is slow to anger is better than the mighty, / And he who rules his spirit than he who takes a city. (Prov. 16:32)

- Guard your ears. The ear is the primary entry point for evil spirits that produce slander, backbiting, gossip, dissension, disunity, and division. "He who goes about as a talebearer reveals secrets; / Therefore do not associate with one who flatters with his lips" (Prov. 20:19).

- Guard your tongue. The tongue can be used to create a breach in the spirit and provide access for the enemy. Watch what you say! "In the multitude of words sin is not lacking, / But he who restrains his lips is wise" (Prov. 10:19).
- Guard your eyes. Pornographic material and violent movies can transfer spirits of adultery, lust, and violence.
- Guard your affections. Do not give your respect and love carelessly to just anyone. Open yourself up emotionally only to those worthy of your trust. "Keep your heart with all diligence, / For out of it spring the issues of life" (Prov. 4:23).
- Carefully select your associates. The book of Proverbs warns repeatedly of the danger of associating with those who have wrong spirits. We are warned:

> Make no friendship with an angry man, / And with a furious man do not go, / Lest you learn his ways / And set a snare for your soul. (Prov. 22:24–25)

> Do not enter the path of the wicked, / And do not walk in the way of evil. / Avoid it, do not travel on it; / Turn away from it and pass on. (Prov. 4:14–15)

> Go from the presence of a foolish man, / When you do not perceive in him the lips of knowledge. (Prov. 14:7)

Likewise, if we walk with wise men their spirits will be transferred to us.

> He who walks with wise men will be wise, / But the companion of fools will be destroyed. (Prov. 13:20)

Choose your close associates carefully. If you are a parent, carefully monitor friends of your children.

- Watch carefully such things as the laying on of hands. Without considering the Scriptures some churches allow everybody in the congregation to lay hands on everybody else. This can be extremely dangerous. We must be assured of the spirit of the individuals who lay hands on others. Getting to know them over a period of time allows us to better discern their spirit.

  The elders laid hands on Timothy: "Do not neglect the gift that is in you, which was given to you by prophecy with the laying on of the hands of the eldership" (1 Tim. 4:14). But Paul wrote to Timothy and told him not to be in a hurry to lay hands on others. "Do not lay hands on anyone hastily, nor share in other people's sins; keep yourself pure" (1 Tim. 5:22).

Do you feel you have been affected by the transference of an evil spirit? Who do you believe influenced your spirit? What were the results of this negative influence?

If you have been affected by the transference of an evil spirit or want to defend against being affected by one, create a plan to follow the strategies discussed in this chapter.

Control your own spirit:

Guard your ears:

Guard your tongue:

Guard your eyes:

Guard your affections:
_____

Carefully select your associates:
_____

Watch carefully such things as the laying on of hands:
_____

13 RESCUE THE WOUNDED

Objectives: Through this strategy session, you will learn to:

- Identify the source of suffering
- List the reasons for suffering
- Develop proper attitudes toward suffering
- Explain the positive benefits of suffering
- Distinguish between the two types of storms of life
- Realize that Christian soldiers sometimes suffer
- Rescue the wounded soldier

Key Verses for This Study:

> Therefore let those who suffer according to the will of God commit their souls to Him in doing good, as to a faithful Creator. (1 Peter 4:19)

> You therefore must endure hardship as a good soldier of Jesus Christ. (2 Tim. 2:3)

Step Thirteen: Rescue the Wounded

Tremendous victory is only possible in the face of a tremendous battle. As we consider affliction, our desire should be to help each other find victory in hidden places and "overcome him by the blood of the Lamb" in very practical moment-by-moment happenings in our day-to-day lives.

—Edith Schaeffer

Warring armies suffer losses: soldiers get wounded. Some recover from their injuries and return to the front, others become permanent casualties.

The same happens with Christian soldiers. We are not immune to the attacks of Satan, nor are we exempt from the effects of suffering.

Because we do not like to talk about pain, we do not hear a great deal of preaching on the subject. We prefer to hear messages on victory and prosperity. Perhaps we avoid the subject of suffering because it is hard to understand and difficult to explain.

But the Bible is not just a book of promises concerning the abundant life. It is also a record of suffering, both of the righteous and the unrighteous.

When Jesus spoke of the suffering He would face on the cross, many of His followers deserted Him (John 6:55-66). They had expected the Messiah to reign in power and glory. Instead, He spoke of trouble and sorrow. Not understanding, they turned away.

If you do not understand suffering, you too may turn from following Jesus when you face difficult circumstances and become a casualty of the war instead of a conqueror.

The Source of Suffering

Suffering, sorrow, and pain entered the world because of sin, but God did not create sin. We created it out of the free will God gave us. Sometimes we are tempted to blame Satan for our sin, but nowhere does God's Word hold him responsible for our wrongdoing. He created his own sin and then tempted us to do the same. Unfortunately, that is exactly what we did.

The Reasons for Suffering

The Bible has much to say concerning suffering and sorrow. In summarizing its teaching, we discover a number of ways that pain can come to the life of a believer.

- *Suffering and sorrow may come through other people.* The story of Joseph shows how this type of suffering can come about. Through no fault of his own, he was sold into slavery in Egypt by his brothers and was later falsely imprisoned because of Potiphar's wife. The actions of other people brought adversity into his life.

  Sometimes suffering comes to the Christian soldier by what the Bible calls an evil report, or gossip. Much hurt comes because of what we say about others, and what they say about us. The tongue is a powerful weapon and can create many casualties of war.
- *Suffering and sorrow come through the circumstances of life.* This is illustrated by the story of Naomi recorded in the book of Ruth. When Naomi was overwhelmed with sorrow and grief at the death of her husband and sons, she said, "Do not call me Naomi [which means 'blessed']; call me Mara [which means 'bitter']" (1:20).

  Until Jesus returns, death will continue to be a part of what happens here on earth. Death entered the world when Adam sinned and is a natural circumstance we all must face. "As it is appointed for men to die once" (Heb. 9:27).
- *Suffering and sorrow come because of faith in Jesus.* The New Testament speaks of suffering for His name's sake (Acts 9:16); in behalf of

Christ (Phil. 1:29); for the kingdom of God (2 Thess. 1:5); for the gospel (2 Tim. 1:11–12); for well doing (1 Peter 2:19–20; 3:17); for righteousness sake (1 Peter 3:14); as a Christian (1 Peter 4:15–16); and according to the will of God (1 Peter 4:19).

The life of the apostle Paul is an example of suffering that resulted from ministry. Some people view all suffering as a sign of failure or of a lack of faith. If this is true, then Paul had no faith and was the greatest failure in the history of the church.

Paul said that while in Asia he was so utterly crushed that he despaired of life itself (2 Cor. 1:8). He presents a different image from that of the cheerful evangelist who promises believers nothing but peace and prosperity.

When Paul was first called by God to ministry he was told of "great things" he would suffer for the sake of the Lord (Acts 9:16 KJV). He endured "the loss of all things to win some [people] for Christ." He wrote the believers in Philippi, "For to you it has been granted on behalf of Christ, not only to believe in Him, but also to suffer for His sake" (Phil. 1:29).

Paul was not alone in suffering for the ministry. The whole church suffered in early New Testament times (see Acts 8:1–3).

Many men and women of faith throughout history have been delivered by the power of God. Prison doors have opened. Sentenced to death in fiery furnaces, some emerged unaffected by the flames.

But some people of faith did not receive such deliverances. They were imprisoned, afflicted, tormented, and even martyred because of their testimony for the gospel (Heb. 11:36–40).

- *Suffering and sorrow come as a result of satanic activity.* The book of Job wrestles with the question, "Why do the righteous suffer?"

God testified that Job was a righteous man (Job 1–2). Job did not suffer because he had sinned, as his friends claimed. On the contrary, he suffered because of his great love for God.

Job's friends tried to make a universal application based on individual experience. Using this logic we could say that because God delivered Peter from prison He will do the same for you. But this is not true. Many have been martyred despite their great faith and holy lives.

We must exercise care in viewing the suffering of others that we do not accuse them of sin, faithlessness, or unbelief. The Bible teaches that a sinful person reaps a bitter harvest (Gal. 6:8). But the principle of sowing and reaping cannot be used to explain the suffering of the righteous.

Job did not suffer because of anything he had done—he was a righteous man. But behind the scenes, in the spiritual world, there was a battle going on over Job's dedication to God. Sometimes God permits stressful situations into our lives in order to toughen us spiritually. Spiritual muscles, like natural ones, only develop through exercise.

An important point made in Job's story of suffering is that nothing can enter the life of a believer without God's knowledge. Although God allows Satan to inflict some suffering in our lives, He does limit it. God's power is greater than Satan's, and we will experience victory if we continue to trust the Lord when the enemy attacks.

- *Sometimes suffering and sorrow come as a result of our own sin.* A good deal of human pain is the result of the law of sowing and reaping. We see such suffering in the story of Jonah. In disobedience to the known will of God, he headed the opposite direction from Nineveh, where he had been commanded to go and preach repentance. Because of his sin, he experienced a terrible storm at sea and ended up in the belly of a great fish (Jonah 1–2).

We should always treat trouble as a call to consider our ways and examine our hearts before God. We may be suffering because of our own sin. If that is the case, we need to humble ourselves before God and repent.

- *Sometimes suffering and sorrow come as a result of God's chastening.* The Bible reveals that God chastises (disciplines or corrects) those who live in disobedience to His Word. "Now no chastening seems to be joyful for the present, but painful; nevertheless, afterward it yields the peaceable fruit of righteousness to those who have been trained by it" (Heb. 12:11). God uses suffering to correct us and bring us back to His will for our lives. "Before I was afflicted I went astray, / But now I keep Your word. . . . It is good for me that I have been afflicted, / That I may learn Your statutes. . . . I know, O LORD, that Your judgments are right, / And that in faithfulness You have afflicted me" (Ps. 119:67, 71, 75).

Are you currently suffering? If so, how?

Review the reasons for suffering discussed in this section. Which reasons might be behind your current suffering? Check those that apply.

- ___ Others around you
- ___ Circumstances of life
- ___ Your faith in Jesus
- ___ Satanic activity
- ___ Your own sin
- ___ God's chastening

If your suffering is due to your own sin, see the biblical remedy in 1 John 1:8–9. You must recognize that you have sinned, confess that sin to God, and ask His forgiveness. If your suffering is caused by any of the other reasons, why might God have allowed it?

Proper Attitudes toward Suffering

As we look at the different reasons for suffering and sorrow we discover that trouble is not necessarily a sign that we are out of God's will. The Bible declares that "many are the afflictions of the righteous" (Ps. 34:19).

Whatever the source of our suffering, we must labor to develop positive attitudes toward people and God. We may find this difficult, but it is vitally necessary.

The real test of spirituality is how we respond in distress. "If you faint in the day of adversity, / Your strength is small" (Prov. 24:10). Be careful not to make too much out of some of the minor difficulties of life. God's Word cautions against lamenting over small things. "If you have run with the footmen, and they have wearied you, / Then how can you contend with horses? / And if in the land of peace, / In which you trusted, they wearied you, / Then how will you do in the floodplain of the Jordan?" (Jer. 12:5).

The Bible describes the attitude we should have when we suffer as believers within the will of God.

- *We should not be ashamed.* "Yet if anyone suffers as a Christian, let him not be ashamed, but let him glorify God in this matter" (1 Peter 4:16). "Therefore do not be ashamed of the testimony of our Lord, nor of me His prisoner, but share with me in the sufferings for the gospel according to the power of God" (2 Tim. 1:8).
- *We should commit our souls to God, knowing He works all things for our good.* "Therefore let those who suffer according to the will of God commit their souls to Him in doing good, as to a faithful Creator" (1 Peter 4:19).
- *We should rejoice when we suffer according to the will of God.* "So they departed from the presence of the council, rejoicing that they were counted worthy to suffer . . . for His name" (Acts 5:41).

- *We should not think it strange when we experience suffering.* "Beloved, do not think it strange concerning the fiery trial which is to try you, as though some strange thing happened to you; but rejoice to the extent that you partake of Christ's sufferings, that when His glory is revealed, you may also be glad with exceeding joy" (1 Peter 4:12–13).

Paul summarized the proper attitude toward suffering:

We are hard pressed on every side, yet not crushed; we are perplexed, but not in despair; persecuted, but not forsaken; struck down, but not destroyed. . . . Therefore we do not lose heart. Even though our outward man is perishing, yet the inward man is being renewed day by day. For our light affliction, which is but for a moment, is working for us a far more exceeding and eternal weight of glory, while we do not look at the things which are seen, but at the things which are not seen. For the things which are seen are temporary, but the things which are not seen are eternal. (2 Cor. 4:8–9, 16–18)

But in all things we commend ourselves as ministers of God: in much patience, in tribulations, in needs, in distresses, in stripes, in imprisonments, in tumults, in labors, in sleeplessness, in fastings. (2 Cor. 6:4–5)

Therefore we make it our aim, whether present or absent, to be well pleasing to Him. For we must all appear before the judgment seat of Christ, that each one may receive the things done in the body, according to what he has done, whether good or bad. (2 Cor. 5:9–10)

For indeed, when we came to Macedonia, our bodies had no rest, but we were troubled on every side. Outside were conflicts, inside were fears. (2 Cor. 7:5)

Analyze your response to suffering by checking the following that apply.

When I suffer . . .

- ___ I maintain a positive attitude toward God
- ___ I maintain a positive attitude toward other people
- ___ I lament over small things
- ___ I am ashamed because others may think I am weak
- ___ I commit my suffering to God, knowing He works all things for my good
- ___ I think it is strange that I should have to suffer
- ___ I easily lose heart

Pray about those areas where you need an attitude adjustment.

Positive Benefits of Suffering

- *Our faith once tested becomes stronger.* Everything we understand about the spiritual world is based on faith (not blind acceptance, but spiritual evidence). True faith, however, only comes through God's Word. To strengthen our faith, God often tests us. "In this you greatly rejoice, though now for a little while, if need be, you have been grieved by various trials, that the genuineness of your faith, being much more precious than gold that perishes, though it is tested by fire, may be found to praise, honor, and glory at the revelation of Jesus Christ" (1 Peter 1:6–7).

  Our faith may be tried when we pray for our difficulties to pass and they do not, forcing us instead to drink more deeply of suffering. Eventually we discover that our prayers did not go unanswered, but God answered in a way we didn't anticipate.

- *God has equipped us to comfort others.* "Blessed be the God and Father of our Lord Jesus Christ, the Father of mercies and God of all comfort, who comforts us in all our tribulation, that we may be able to comfort those who are in any trouble, with the comfort with which we ourselves are comforted by God" (2 Cor. 1:3-4).

    Therefore strengthen the hands which hang down, and the feeble knees, and make straight paths for your feet, so that what is lame may not be dislocated, but rather be healed. (Heb. 12:12-13)

- *We learn not to trust in ourselves.* Paul spoke of the purpose of his sufferings: "For we do not want you to be ignorant, brethren, of our trouble which came to us in Asia: that we were burdened beyond measure, above strength, so that we despaired even of life. Yes, we had the sentence of death in ourselves, that we should not trust in ourselves but in God who raises the dead" (2 Cor. 1:8-9).

    Paul came to recognize that ". . .we have this treasure in earthen vessels, that the excellence of the power may be of God and not of us" (2 Cor. 4:7).
- *We develop positive spiritual qualities.* "And not only that, but we also glory in tribulations, knowing that tribulation produces perseverance; and perseverance, character; and character, hope" (Rom. 5:3-4). "But may the God of all grace, who called us to His eternal glory by Christ Jesus, after you have suffered a while, perfect, establish, strengthen, and settle you" (1 Peter 5:10). These qualities conform us to the image of Jesus, which is God's ultimate plan (see Rom. 8:28-29 and Heb. 2:10, 18).
- *The works of God are manifested to us.* When the disciples saw a man who was blind from birth, they asked Jesus who was responsible for his condition. Was it the sin of his parents or of the man himself?

> Jesus answered, "Neither this man nor his parents sinned, but that the works of God should be revealed in him." (John 9:3)

This man's condition was not due to sin. God had a special plan to demonstrate His healing power by healing this man's affliction.

- *God perfects His power in us.* "And He said to me, 'My grace is sufficient for you, for My strength is made perfect in weakness.' Therefore most gladly I will rather boast in my infirmities, that the power of Christ may rest upon me" (2 Cor. 12:9).
- *God removes that which is unstable.* Suffering results in all that is unstable being shaken out of our lives. We cease to depend so much on people, programs, or material things as these all fail in our time of need.

  God permits "the removal of those things that are being shaken, as of things that are made, that the things which cannot be shaken may remain" (Heb. 12:27). During the storms of life, everything crumbles that is not built upon God and His Word.
- *Our focus is changed.* When we experience suffering, we often focus our attention on cause and effect. We think about what caused our difficult circumstances and their terrible effects in our lives, often asking, "Why did this happen to me?" Often we become too occupied with self-pity and insult that arise from such internal statements as, "Pain had no right to touch me."

  God changes our focus from our own self-centered needs, pains, problems, and desires to an understanding of and a commitment to eternal values: "For our light affliction, which is but for a moment, is working for us a far more exceeding and eternal weight of glory, while we do not look at the things which are seen, but at the things which are not seen. For the things which are seen are temporary, but the things which are not seen are eternal" (2 Cor. 4:17–18). "Beloved, do not think it strange concerning the fiery trial which is to try you, as though some strange thing happened to you; but rejoice to the extent that you partake of Christ's sufferings, that when His glory is revealed, you may also be glad with exceeding joy" (1 Peter 4:12–13).

- *The old self-nature changes.* God said of the nation of Moab: "Moab has been at ease from his youth; / He has settled on his dregs, / And has not been emptied from vessel to vessel, / Nor has he gone into captivity. / Therefore his taste remained in him, / And his scent has not changed" (Jer. 48:11).

  Because Moab was at ease and settled in prosperity, the nation did not develop and mature in a proper spiritual manner. But suffering rids us of our old self-nature. As we are stirred by the troubles of life, God changes us from carnal to spiritual.

- *We are prepared for ministry.* We ask God to use us. We desire to be more like Jesus and pray to be chosen vessels for His use. Sometimes God answers our prayers by sending suffering. "Behold, I have refined you, but not as silver; / I have tested you in the furnace of affliction" (Isa. 48:10).

  Through affliction, we move beyond the calling as a "child of God" to become "chosen of God." Affliction, according to the will of God, refines us for His use just as metals are refined and purified in a furnace.

  God actually prepares us through suffering to wage warfare against the enemy!

- *We are prepared to reign with Christ.* "If we endure, / We shall also reign with Him" (2 Tim. 2:12).

- *We receive spiritual blessings.* Jesus said:

  Blessed are those who are persecuted for righteousness' sake, / For theirs is the kingdom of heaven. / Blessed are you when they revile and persecute you, and say all kinds of evil against you falsely for My sake. Rejoice and be exceedingly glad, for great is your reward in heaven, for so they persecuted the prophets who were before you. (Matt. 5:10-12)

- *We learn obedience.* "Though He was a Son, yet He learned obedience by the things which He suffered" (Heb. 5:8).
- *The Word of God is tested within us.* "The words of the LORD are pure words, / Like silver tried in a furnace of earth, / Purified seven times" (Ps. 12:6).
- *We are humbled.*

> Who led you through that great and terrible wilderness, in which were fiery serpents and scorpions and thirsty land where there was no water; who brought water for you out of the flinty rock; who fed you in the wilderness with manna, which your fathers did not know, that He might humble you and that He might test you, to do you good in the end. (Deut. 8:15-16)

- *We are increased spiritually.* This means we grow spiritually. "Thou hast enlarged me when I was in distress" (Ps. 4:1 KJV).
- *We come to know God intimately.* God often comes very close to those who have suffered. Job learned this truth and said: "I have heard of You by the hearing of the ear, / But now my eye sees You. / Therefore I abhor myself, / And repent in dust and ashes" (Job 42:5-6).

Some of us know God on a secondhand basis. When we experience the blessings of life, we often see God as a luxury rather than a necessity. But when we suffer real pain, we suddenly need Him.

Job came to know the Lord more intimately through his trials. Before he suffered, much of what he knew of God was theological. Afterward, he knew Him personally.

Paul's trials caused him to want to know Christ all the more. "That I may know Him and the power of His resurrection, and the fellowship of His sufferings, being conformed to His death" (Phil. 3:10).

We can only come to know God in resurrection power through the intimate fellowship of suffering.

In his pain, Job questioned God as to the cause of his trouble.

Even Jesus asked questions of the Father. He knew He came into the world to die for the sins of all. Yet in His hour of suffering He cried, "My God, My God, why have you forsaken me?" It is not wrong to ask God why things happen. It is wrong, however, to question His right to allow adversity into our lives.

What follows our questions is vital. Jesus' next words were, "Into thy hands I commit my spirit."

And despite his questions, Job responded, "Though He slay me, yet will I trust Him" (Job 13:15). "For I know that my Redeemer lives, / And He shall stand at last on the earth; / And after my skin is destroyed, this I know, / That in my flesh I shall see God" (Job 19:25-26).

After our questioning, the emphasis must change from "me" to "Thee." You must commit your suffering, with all its unanswered questions, into the hands of God. "Trust in the LORD with all your heart, and lean not on your own understanding" (Prov. 3:5).

While God may reveal some of the purposes in your suffering He may not reveal all of them because "the secret things belong to the LORD our God, but those things which are revealed belong to us and to our children forever, that we may do all the words of this law" (Deut. 29:29).

When God answered Job, He asked Job to explain some of the natural things occurring around him. Job could not. God then stressed that if Job could not understand what he saw in the natural world, he certainly could not understand that which he could not see in the spiritual world.

When Job faced God, it no longer mattered that he did not get an answer to his questions about suffering. He was in the presence of God, and that was all that mattered. He was no longer controlled and tormented by human reasoning. Questions were replaced, not with answers, but with God.

When we come to know God intimately through suffering, we see ourselves as we really are. A face-to-face encounter with God does what arguments and discussions cannot do.

Analyze the suffering you have experienced. What positive benefits have resulted from your suffering?

___ Having my faith tested and made stronger
___ Being equipped to comfort others
___ Learning not to trust in myself
___ Developing positive spiritual qualities
___ Manifesting the works of God
___ Having the power of God perfected in me
___ Removing that which is unstable
___ Changing my focus
___ Changing my old self-nature
___ Preparing me for ministry
___ Preparing me to reign with Christ
___ Receiving spiritual blessings
___ Learning obedience
___ Testing the Word of God within me
___ Being humbled
___ Increasing spiritually
___ Coming to know God intimately

The Storms of Life

Suffering is sometimes compared to a natural storm. When we suffer, we experience an inner disturbance that may affect us spiritually, mentally, physically, or emotionally.

Once when Jesus and His disciples crossed a lake to the region of the Gerasenes, a violent storm arose and nearly swamped the boat. The disciples woke Jesus, who slept in the back of the boat, and asked, "Teacher, don't you care if we drown?" Immediately Jesus took authority over the tempest. He commanded the violent wind to stop and calm returned to the sea. They continued their journey unhindered.

Many kinds of storms arise in life. In a storm of Satan, the enemy tries to hinder us from fulfilling the will of God. The suffering that results is neither from disobedience nor necessarily "according to the will of God." When we face this type of storm, we must exercise the authority Jesus has given us over the power of Satan.

Read the story of Jonah's storm in Jonah 1 and the story of Paul and the storm in Acts 27. These stories illustrate suffering by chastisement for sin and suffering according to the will of God. Then study the following comparisons.

Jonah	Paul
Jonah put himself in the storm. He paid the fare.	Paul was in the storm through no fault of his own. He tried to prevent them from sailing.
Jonah was the cause of the storm.	Paul was the remedy to the storm.
Jonah slept during the storm.	Paul fasted and prayed in the storm.

Jonah	Paul
God's blessing was not with Jonah.	God's blessing was with Paul.
The crew was fearful.	The crew was of good cheer.
To be saved: Jonah must be cast out of the ship.	To be saved: All must abide in the ship.

Do you see the difference between going through a storm of life within God's will and experiencing a storm out of His will? When we go through a storm out of the will of God, we have generally created the situation through sin. We cause the storms that result from disobedience by violating God's will and His commands. Often we are not aware of the seriousness of our situation because we sleep spiritually while the storm rages around us.

When we fully recognize the storm that results from disobeying God's voice, we have only one remedy: ask Him for forgiveness!

But when we suffer according to the will of God, the situation is different. The suffering does not come as the result of our sin. In such circumstances, we must simply weather the storm. We must not bail out of the ship or run from trouble. We must abide in this "ship of suffering," for it is the will of God. Eventually, He will bring us safely to a calm harbor.

The Suffering Soldier

Many storms of life are inevitable and uncontrollable. Read the parable of the two houses in Matthew 7:24-27. Storms come to those who build their lives upon God's Word as well as those who do not. But the foundation of a person's life will determine the outcome of the storm.

When you suffer according to the will of God, you are not alone. Many others in God's army have experienced similar situations. "The same sufferings are experienced by your brotherhood in the world" (1 Peter 5:9).

We must expect (but not seek) suffering as part of the will of God. And much of our suffering will come as persecution. "Yes, and all who desire to live godly in Christ Jesus will suffer persecution" (2 Tim. 3:12).

In the early church, believers were taught that they would experience suffering. "Strengthening the souls of the disciples, exhorting them to continue in the faith, and saying, 'We must through many tribulations enter the kingdom of God'" (Acts 14:22). This is missing in many churches today. The call to follow Jesus *is* a call to denial and suffering. "Then Jesus said to His disciples, 'If anyone desires to come after Me, let him deny himself, and take up his cross, and follow Me'" (Matt. 16:24).

You must never make yourself suffer, believing it would be pleasing to God. God is never pleased when people suffer. He only allows suffering for the good it can bring. To purposefully make ourselves to suffer (an act called asceticism) is a grievous sin. Many people do this to appease God's anger. But God's anger is only appeased through the shed blood of His Son Jesus. We can make peace with God by accepting Jesus into our lives.

For further study look up the following Scriptures: Phil. 1:29; 2 Thess. 1:5; 1 Thess. 3:4; Matt. 24:9; Luke 21:12; John 15:20; Matt. 10:38; Mark 8:34; Luke 9:23; Luke 14:27.

Rescuing the Wounded

Soldiers help one another in battle. They fire their weapons at the enemy to provide cover so the one under attack can run to safety. Do you know of a wounded warrior, a casualty of war for whom you can provide such spiritual cover? Identify the person and write out a plan.

_____
_____
_____

14 DELIVER THE DEMONIZED

Objectives: Through this strategy session, you will learn to:

- Cite biblical examples of the reality of demons
- Understand who should deal with demonic forces
- Detect the presence of demons
- Use the methods of Jesus
- Summarize the guidelines for dealing with demons
- Prepare yourself to deliver the demonized
- Prepare others to deliver the demonized
- Determine the place for ministry to the demonized
- Minister deliverance
- Recognize signs of deliverance
- Provide follow-up care

Key Verses for This Study:

> Jesus asked him, saying, "What is your name?" And he said, "Legion," because many demons had entered him. And they begged Him that He would not command them to go out into the abyss. (Luke 8:30–31)

> And these signs will follow those who believe: In My name they will cast out demons. (Mark 16:17)

And when He had called His twelve disciples to Him, He gave them power over unclean spirits, to cast them out, and to heal all kinds of sickness and all kinds of disease. (Matt. 10:1)

Heal the sick, cleanse the lepers, raise the dead, cast out demons. (Matt. 10:8)

And He called the twelve to Himself, and began to send them out two by two, and gave them power over unclean spirits. (Mark 6:7)

Step Fourteen: Deliver the Demonized

Satan cannot stand an exposition of the blood of Christ. He turns pale at every view of Calvary. The flowing wounds are the signal of his retreat. A heart besprinkled with the blood is holy ground, on which he not only dares not tread, but he dreads and trembles and cowers in the presence of the blood-besprinkled warrior. A clear-ringing word of testimony to the power of that blood he fears more than the attack of a legion of archangels. It is like the charge of an irresistible phalanx which bears everything down before it. It is the blood applied, and the testimony to its application, the martyr witness in life and by tongue of the power of that blood is more a barrier to Satan than a wall of fire.

—E. M. Bounds

To wage effective warfare, we must learn how to deal with the demonic powers that affect the lives of people. This chapter presents guidelines for ministering to those troubled by demons.

Biblical Examples of the Reality of Demons

Perhaps the best-known story of demon possession in the Bible is the account of the man from Gadarenes. Jesus had gone to the area by boat and as He stepped ashore He met a naked man who had been living in the tombs. When the man saw Jesus he cried out, "What have I to do with You, Jesus, Son of the Most High God? I beg You, do not torture me!"

> And Jesus asked him, saying, "What is your name?" And he said, "Legion," because many demons had entered him. And they begged Him that He would not command them to go out into the abyss. Now a herd of many swine was feeding there on the mountain. And they begged Him that He would permit them to enter them. And He permitted them. Then the demons went out of the man and entered the swine, and the herd ran violently down the steep place into the lake and drowned. (Luke 8:30–33)

Other accounts of people affected by demons are documented in Matthew 9:32–33; 12:22; Mark 9:14–29.

Perhaps one of the greatest, yet ludicrous, arguments against the reality of demon spirits comes from those in Christian nations, sometimes from Christian leaders. The lack of demonic manifestations in these lands in contrast to the overwhelming evidence of them in many pagan lands has led some people to question their existence despite the biblical record. In the 1940s Dr. Rudolf Bultmamn, a noted New Testament scholar, scoffed at the idea of angels and demons. Such nonbiblical views have spawned fierce debate. The reality of demons, however, is observed not only in biblical accounts but also in contemporary cases.[1]

Who Should Deal with Demonic Forces?

Dealing with demons need not be left only to professional ministers. Jesus said all mature believers would have the ability to overcome demonic powers. "And these signs will follow those who believe: In My name they will cast out demons" (Mark 16:17). He first delegated this power to the disciples. "And when He had called His twelve disciples to Him, He gave them power over unclean spirits, to cast them out, and to heal all kinds of sickness and all kinds of disease" (Matt. 10:1).

While there is no biblical basis for believing that God intended to restrict this important ministry to a particular group of people, we should not rush into encounters with the enemy without proper preparation, as the sons of Sceva did (Acts 19).[2] *Only under the guidance of the Holy Spirit* should we seek to fulfill this kind of ministry.

We must also take care that we not become overly demon conscious. God has not called us to "major" in demons. Our highest calling is to exalt Jesus.

However, we should not fear demon spirits. When confronted with oppressed or possessed people, we have the power from God to bring deliverance.

What attitude have you taken toward dealing with demonic forces?

___ Ignored them
___ Feared them
___ Recognized them, but did not act
___ Recognized the forces and dealt with them in spiritual battle

How might your response differ in the future when you come in contact with demonic forces?

_____
_____

Detecting the Presence of Demons

To overcome demons we must be able to recognize their presence and tactics. The Holy Spirit has provided a special spiritual gift for this purpose. This gift is called "discerning of spirits" (1 Cor. 12:10).

The gift of discerning of spirits enables a believer to identify the presence of a demon. This is necessary because identification is not always easy. At times mental illness and demon possession have similar characteristics.

For example, sometimes deafness and muteness are caused by a spirit (according to the biblical record). Other times they might be the result of an accident or illness. Discernment enables a person to determine the cause behind the condition.

In many cases, we can make preliminary diagnosis by observing the actions of individuals. When the Canaanite woman came to Jesus with an appeal that He cast out an evil spirit from her daughter, she said, "My daughter is severely demon-possessed" (Matt. 15:22). How did she know this? She recognized the symptoms.

But we must take extreme care to assure proper identification. We can cause severe damage by suggesting the presence of a demon when in fact there is none or by properly suggesting there is one without giving the person involved some hope for deliverance.

Earlier we discussed how to recognize demons (see Chapter 12). You might want to review that lesson before proceeding.

The Methods of Jesus

Let's examine three cases that illustrate the methods Jesus used in dealing with demons.

1. Consider the man attending the local synagogue in Capernaum when Jesus was present (Mark 1:21–28).

a. Unlike the scribes, Jesus taught with authority (verse 22).
   b. The man became overwhelmed by the unclean spirit influencing him and he cried out during the service (verses 23–24).
   c. Jesus told the spirit to be quiet and come out (verse 25).
   d. The spirit convulsed, the man cried out, and the spirit left (verse 26).
   e. The people were shocked and amazed because of the unparalled authority exercised by Jesus in their midst (verses 27–28).
2. Consider the Gadarene demoniac (Mark 5:1–20).
   a. He was greatly tormented (verses 2–5).
   b. He saw Jesus, ran, and worshiped Him. Notice that no matter how demonized someone is, the will can still move toward deliverance from bondage (verse 6).
   c. Demonic influence took over and challenged Jesus. One demon spoke for all others present (verse 7).
   d. Jesus went through a process of expelling the demons. The chief demon was possibly quite resistant. The Greek word *saying* in the phrase "Jesus was saying to him" is imperfect in form and connotes a continual action (verses 8–10).
   e. The ex-demoniac was glad to be set free (verses 15, 18, 20).
   f. Jesus told the ex-demoniac to stay there and tell his friends about what the Lord had done for him, and how He had mercy on him (verse 19).
3. Consider the woman who was bent over and could not straighten up for eighteen years (Luke 13:10–17).
   a. Jesus called her a daughter of Abraham (verse 16).
   b. Jesus discerned that she "had a spirit of infirmity" and had been bound by Satan for eighteen years (verses 11, 16).

    c. Jesus said to her, "Woman, you are loosed from your infirmity." He then put his hands on her, and immediately she straightened up and praised God (verses 12–13).
    d. The woman and the common people were glad, but the religious leaders were angry (verses 13, 14, 17).

Notice several common threads in the stories of Jesus dealing with demons:

- His presence stirred them up, and they manifested in unmistakable ways so they could be dealt with.
- Jesus spoke to the demons in a powerful encounter and commanded them to leave.
- The demonized person was set free.

Summarize what you have learned from these three examples about how Jesus dealt with demons.
_____
_____
_____

Guidelines for Dealing with Demons

Here are some suggestions for dealing with demons:

- *Pray for discernment.* Demons must be dealt with only on the basis of Jesus' authority. Do not attempt deliverance outside of His guidance.
- *Recognize the symptoms.* (See "Recognizing Demon Spirits" in Chapter 12.) Diagnosing demonization is a skill learned through practice and aided by discernment. Often you will observe two or more symptoms in the person involved.

- *Be slow to make judgments.* A misdiagnosis can be damaging.
- *Recognize the person as well as the demon(s).* In your anger against the demon(s), don't forget to be sensitive to the person.
- *Do not deal with the situation alone.* Demonized people sometimes exhibit incredible strength. You will less likely be intimidated and deceived by their cunning if several other people assist you (we recommend four to six people). Some should pray while others work with the situation.
- *Recognize tactics.* See "The Ministry of Deliverance" section of this chapter.
- *Do not be afraid.* If you know Jesus personally you have the assurance that "greater is He that is in you, than he that is in the world" (1 John 4:4 KJV).
- *Keep what you discover confidential.* That the person was ever affected can be a great source of embarrassment.
- *Continue to minister to the individual after the demons have left.* Good instruction will help the person resist the enemy properly. If you cannot continue ministry see that someone else does.
- *Do not be discouraged by an apparent failure.* Deliverance for some may come in stages. Several sessions may be necessary to get things "cleaned up."
- *Do not be distracted by extreme fatigue while dealing with demons.* Eight hours of hard labor may come easier than one hour with a demonized person.
- *Be ready to stay for an extended period of time.* It may take many hours for a person to be delivered.
- *Remember your weapons.* The name of Jesus and the blood of the Lamb are primary elements in casting out demons. We studied these in Chapter 8. Recall that the name of Jesus signifies power through invested authority while the blood of Jesus serves as a legal document, which we hold up before God to claim legal access to the throne and before Satan's demons to claim release from their power.

- *Be on guard yourself for several days after you have been in a session.* Be especially sensitive to your thought patterns. Resist all attacks tenaciously. If necessary, get help. Ask brothers and sisters in Christ to pray for you if you sense trouble.
- *Watch for distractions.* Demons will make noises, cry, and carry on in various ways to distract you. Some may say, "This is my house, I'm not leaving." Also be on guard for their deceptions. For instance, they may say, "They're gone, I'm free," making you think they have been cast out. When they are gone, you will know it. There will be an obvious change in the person involved.
- *Keep in mind that demons are afraid of Christians who walk with Jesus.*

Personal Preliminary Preparations

Faith comes by hearing the Word of God. Begin to build faith in your heart by reading the New Testament with a new attitude.

Whatever Jesus told His followers to do, begin to do. Whatever He said He would do, expect Him to do it. If He said you can deliver those afflicted by Satan, then expect to see them delivered. If He said to cast out devils, then do it in His name and expect them to obey you, but do this *only* under the direction of the Holy Spirit.

Accept that the New Testament means exactly what it says. Accept it as true and act accordingly.

You are an ambassador for Christ (2 Cor. 5:20). Never doubt that He will back up His word.

When possible, fast and pray *before* you go to minister deliverance. Since power and authority for deliverance come from God, we must be in close touch with Him. Some demons will come out only through praying and fasting. Isaiah 58 teaches that God honors the fast that focuses on ministering to the needs of others. Read this chapter and summarize its teachings regarding fasting.

_____

_____

Prepare Others to Deliver the Demonized

Whenever possible, assemble a team of believers to bind or cast out demons. Jesus sent out His disciples in pairs for this ministry: "And He called the twelve to Himself, and began to send them out two by two, and gave them power over unclean spirits" (Mark 6:7).

This does not mean you cannot minister alone when you encounter a demonized person, but there is strength in unity of prayer with another believer. Since strength comes from unity, those who are joining you in the ministry of deliverance should also prepare through praying and fasting.

In cases of oppression and obsession, prepare the person to receive the ministry. He or she needs to have faith built through the Word of God concerning deliverance. (This may not be possible in the case of possession).

When sharing the gospel, a wise soul winner does not press for a decision too quickly. Preliminary ministry must be done, and proper instruction must be given. The same is true of deliverance. Sometimes, God delivers without such instruction. But in ministering deliverance, we want to properly use every channel prescribed by God's Word to see the work done. Faith is one channel for God's delivering power, and it comes by hearing God's Word. That's why instruction is important.

Jesus combined preaching and teaching with healing and deliverance, and He instructed His followers to do so also. When He sent the disciples out, He told them to preach the gospel, heal the sick, and cast out demons.

The Place for Ministry

The ministry of deliverance to those affected by demon spirits need not be confined to private sessions but can be part of the church service. However, because of the need for counseling and because the amount of time required usually exceeds the length of a normal service, it is often best to move a person into another part of the church, away from the main sanctuary.

Jesus ministered to the demon possessed as part of a regular church service (Mark 1:21-25), but you need not wait until a regular service to deal with demonic powers.

Does your church minister to the demonized? How, when, and where?

_____
_____

Can you think of improvements in the time, place, and procedures of such ministry in your church?

_____
_____

The Ministry of Deliverance

When you are ready to minister deliverance . . .

1. *Begin with worship and praise.* We enter His presence (where deliverance and healing take place) through worship and praise. Deliverance can come through worship and praise, even without ministry by prayer, because God inhabits the praises of His people.
2. *Create an environment of faith.* Unbelief hindered the ministry of Jesus in Nazareth, so sometimes Jesus put unbelievers out of the room when He ministered (Mark 5:35–40). At other times, He led people out of their village (an environment of unbelief) in order to minister to them (Mark 8:23). On occasion, as God leads, you may need to ask those struggling with unbelief or fear to leave.
3. *Pray.* Ask for wisdom and discernment before you begin to minister deliverance. During prayer, God may reveal:

   A word of knowledge: Specific facts and information about a person or condition so you will know how to pray. This can include a deep sense of knowing or an impression in your spirit, and it may reveal what the sickness is or why the person has the condition.

   A Scripture verse: The *rhema* word for that situation, condition, person, or group.

   A vision: Pictures in the mind's eye pertaining to the one to whom you minister.

   Words of faith: Special words of encouragement and faith specifically for that individual.

   A special anointing: A sudden infusion of power.

4. *Conduct a brief interview:* This is optional and should be done according to the leading of the Lord. If God gives you specific

words of wisdom about the person's condition, you will not need to conduct an interview.

But if God does not reveal something to you, do not hesitate to ask questions. Jesus used both natural and supernatural methods. On occasions He discerned people's conditions by the Holy Spirit. At other times He asked them what they wanted and how long they had been afflicted.

An interview can help you gain information, so you can pray more specifically. It also helps you determine whether the person needs further instruction before you pray.

Jesus often asked people questions concerning their faith. He then dealt with negative elements of unbelief before ministering.

Study the following examples:

Jesus questions the demonized man: Mark 5:1-20
Jesus questions the blind man: Mark 8:22-26
Jesus questions the father of a boy with an evil spirit: Mark 9:14-27
Jesus questions blind Bartimaeus: Mark 10:46-52

Ask the person, "What is the problem?" A request for prayer from the afflicted is important. Jesus delivered many after they acknowledged their needs. Ask for a specific statement. You need only brief facts. You do not need a complete history or a life's story.

Do not try to analyze the information you receive. Your function is only to minister deliverance. Some cases may require privacy and more time for counseling with an experienced counselor.

Ask the person, "Do you believe Jesus can deliver you?" If the answer is yes, then ask, "Do you believe Jesus will do it now?"

If you receive a no answer to either of these questions, the person needs further instruction from God's Word.

5. *Determine the specific problem.* Use the information from the interview and/or the wisdom God has given to you to determine if the problem is in the:

Spiritual realm: Problems related to sin. These require the ministry of salvation, repentance, and forgiveness of sin.

Physical realm: Bodily sickness caused by demonic spirits of infirmity.

Mental realm: Problems stemming from negative thinking, attacks of Satan on the mind, mental retardation.

Emotional realm: Problems concerning anxiety, fear, anger, bitterness, resentment, guilt, doubt, failure, jealousy, selfishness, confusion, frustration, perfectionism in the energy of the flesh, and unforgiveness.

Deliverance in the emotional realm is often referred to as "inner healing," but this term has been abused. It is not necessary to rehearse in detail past emotional experiences, nor must a person spend weeks, months, or years to recover from such traumas. If you do this, you are trying to heal the old person instead of helping the afflicted become a new creation in Christ.

Problems in the emotional realm are often related to the social realm of a person's life; they affect and stem from family and social relationships. Deliverance comes through identifying the problem, asking forgiveness, and forgiving the other parties involved.

The greatest barrier to emotional healing generally comes in the area of unforgiveness, so emotional healing includes the healing of social relationships.

We are called to be ministers of reconciliation (2 Cor. 5:18–21). You may need to instruct the person in forgiveness. It is *not:*

- Justifying someone else's wrongdoings
- Denying we were hurt in the first place
- Accepting with resignation what was done to us
- Waiting for time to heal the hurt

True forgiveness comes by:

- Recognizing what was done to us was wrong.
- Confessing the hurt to God and asking Him to heal the harmful emotions. You may not ever forget the incident but that is OK. What you need is healing for the *wrong emotions* related to it.
- Asking God to help you forgive others, then forgiving even as Christ forgives you. Recognize that God extends forgiveness to you as you forgive others: "Forgive us our trespasses *as* we forgive those who trespass against us."
- Acknowledging the sin that causes the *guilt* and/or sinful emotions, confessing it to God, and repenting. Ask Him to forgive your sin and heal your emotions.
- Recognizing that when God forgives, He does not bring it up again.
- Claiming 1 John 1:8–9 and Romans 8:1.
- Acting of your own will, releasing yourself from condemnation and controlling future thought patterns by taking "captive every thought to make it obedient to Christ" (2 Cor. 10:5 NIV).

Remember, because we are triune beings, problems in one realm affect the whole person. As you minister, deal with the whole person—body, soul, and spirit.

>   6. *Determine the proper time to pray.* In most cases, you will pray, but do not be surprised if the Lord directs you *not* to pray or to *delay* praying.

DELIVER THE DEMONIZED

Jesus delayed healing in the case of the Syrophonecian woman's daughter and Lazarus. He did not do many works at all in Nazareth because of unbelief.

The Lord may also direct you to delay prayer until you or the person you are ministering to receives further instruction.

7. *Pray the prayer of deliverance:* Pray a prayer of deliverance that focuses on the specific problem of demonic influence you have identified.

You do not have to *persuade* God to deliver by your prayer. Just as salvation is readily available and is based on faith, so is deliverance. Sometimes the power of God is present in a special way for deliverance (Luke 5:17), but we can always pray for deliverance because Jesus commanded us to do so.

Use others to help you minister in a group setting. There is multiplication of spiritual power when more people pray (Matt. 18:19). And "body ministry" discourages giving glory to individuals.

Jesus taught that first you should bind the enemy, then you exercise power over him. We have the authority to cast out demons only in the name of Jesus. We have no authority of our own. Remember to use the name (authority) of Jesus in the actual casting out prayer.

You don't need to yell at the demons. Your authority in the name of Jesus will cause them to come out, not the volume of your voice during the prayer of deliverance.

Finally, forbid the demons to reenter the person. This is an important part of the prayer of deliverance. "When Jesus saw that the people came running together, He rebuked the unclean spirit, saying to it, 'Deaf and dumb spirit, I command you, come out of him, and enter him no more!'" (Mark 9:25).

Do not spend time talking with demons, should they manifest through spoken words. Jesus rebuked demons and told them to be quiet (Luke 4:34–35). Remember that any conversation with demons is dangerous because they are lying spirits.

The Holy Spirit will direct you in the prayer of deliverance, but if you are new to this ministry here is a sample prayer to study:

"By the authority of Jesus Christ, His name, His power, His Word, His blood, and the Holy Spirit"

This establishes the power base for deliverance.

"I bind you"

Jesus taught us to bind demons first before attempting to cast them out.

"and I command you"

Ministering deliverance is a prayer of authority, not of entreaty. You can speak quietly, but you must take authority over the forces of evil in the name of Jesus. Look directly into the eyes of the person as you speak.

"spirit of _____"
    or
"you foul spirit of Satan"

If the spirit has been identified either through spiritual or natural discernment, then name it specifically; otherwise, name it generally.

"to depart"

This is the casting out process.

"without harming _____ or anyone in this house, and without creating noise or a disturbance."

Sometimes the demon will try to harm the person or create a disturbance.

"I forbid you to reenter this person"

Remember that Jesus used this command.

"and I ask the Holy Spirit to fill this person and cleanse him/her through the power of the blood of Jesus."

We are told to loosen as well as bind. If you have identified a specific spirit at work, loose the opposite spirit. For example, bind the spirit of pride and loosen the spirit of humility.

"I further forbid you to touch anything related to _____ or myself, or anyone in this house."

Do not make a show of your ministry by allowing crowds to gather. When Jesus saw the actions of a demon attracting a crowd, He immediately stopped the performance being staged by the evil spirit and cast it out.

Do not attempt to cast demons into hell. Jesus and His disciples did not do this. We have authority only to bind, loose, and cast out. There is a set time for the final judgment of demons.

You can pray for those affected by demons with or without the laying on of hands. Jesus laid hands on the woman oppressed with the spirit of infirmity in Luke 13:11-13. In other cases, He simply spoke to the demons (Luke 9:42).

8. *Praise God for the answer.* Follow prayer with praise to God for deliverance. Remember that in the biblical example of the

ten lepers, all were healed, but only the one who returned to praise was made whole (Luke 17:17–19).

Praise by faith and not by sight. You have done what God's Word said to do. Believe He has done what He said He would do, and thank Him for it.

Signs of Deliverance

In cases of demon possession, sometimes the demons come out with a struggle. When demons have departed (whether in possession or oppression), the person involved will feel a sense of release like the lifting of a weight.

Have you ever seen a demonized person delivered? If so, what additional signs of deliverance did you note?

Follow-Up Care

After deliverance, those who have been possessed by demons should be led in a prayer of confession, and repentance, renouncing any sins or involvements connected with demonic activities. If the person has any occult items (for example idols, voodoo materials, witchcraft equipment, etc.), destroy them.

Follow-up care is important because when he is cast out, a demon will seek another body through which to operate. Jesus taught that the departure of evil spirits leaves an empty place. There is danger of a demon returning to his former victim accompanied by worse spirits:

> When an unclean spirit goes out of a man, he goes through dry places, seeking rest; and finding none, he says, "I will return to my house from which I came." And when he comes, he finds it swept and put in order. Then he goes and takes with him seven other spirits more wicked than himself, and they enter and dwell there; and the last state of that man is worse than the first. (Luke 11:24-26)

When cast out, a demon will become restless and discontent. Only by indwelling and controlling a human being can a demon fulfill Satan's evil purposes.

This is why casting the demon out is not enough. The spiritual house must be filled by the new birth experience and the Holy Spirit. Follow-up counseling and ministry are necessary. The person should be immersed in the Word of God and prayer and encouraged to become part of a community of believers.

Encourage those who have experienced deliverance from demonic powers to give their testimony. Jesus told the demoniac of Gadarene, "'Go home to your friends, and tell them what great things the Lord has done for you, and how He has had compassion on you.' And he departed and began to proclaim in Decapolis all that Jesus had done for him; and all marveled" (Mark 5:19-20).

Summarize the eight steps for ministering deliverance discussed in this strategy session.

1.

2.

3.

4.

5.

6.

7.

8.

Having received these basic guidelines for delivering the demonized, continue your study of how Jesus dealt with demon powers by analyzing the following incidents.

Incident: Woman in the synagogue with the spirit of infirmity (Luke 13:10-17)

Summary: This woman attended Sabbath day services and Jesus called her a "daughter of Abraham." We can assume she was a righteous, God-fearing person. Yet a spirit of infirmity had bound her for eighteen years.

Jesus distinguished between normal physical illnesses, which were cured by laying on of hands or anointing with oil, and cases of demon affliction. In cases of a believer being bound as a result of demon affliction, Jesus loosed the binding spirit. If an unbeliever had physical infirmities resulting from demon possession, Jesus cast the demons out.

The deliverance of this woman occurred during a regular church service. In this deliverance, Jesus laid hands on the bound woman. Immediately, she was made straight and glorified God. This prompted opposition from the spiritual leaders, including the ruler of the synagogue.

Dealing with demon powers still raises objections from many spiritual leaders today. Some deny the existence of demons. Others deny their power to oppress or possess.

In all true ministry to demon oppressed or possessed people, God should receive the glory, not the person used of God in the deliverance process. (Note: Church services are not to be disrupted, even for ministry purposes by people not recognized in the leadership of the local assembly without permission by the pastor or other official.)

Incident: The Syrophoenician woman's daughter (Matt. 15:21–28; Mark 7:24–30)

Summary: This young girl had an unclean spirit which her mother recognized by outward manifestations of the spirit. She described her daughter as being "grievously vexed."

Jesus healed the girl because of the great faith shown by her mother. The daughter never entered the presence of Jesus, which demonstrates that actual physical presence is not necessary for effective ministry to those oppressed or possessed by Satan.

This and the following incident prove children can be possessed and oppressed by Satan.

Incident: The deaf mute boy (Matt. 17:14–21; Mark 9:14–29; Luke 9:37–43)

Summary: The father of an only son sought healing for his child from Jesus. The demon possession of this boy included deafness and the inability to speak. The combined descriptions of Matthew, Mark, and Luke reveal that the demon sorely vexed the boy, causing him to fall into the fire and water.

At times the demon tore at him and caused fits that included foaming at the mouth and teeth grinding. He was often bruised (injured) by the spirit, and the demonic presence caused a general physical pining away. His father called him a lunatic, which may indicate there were also mental problems associated with his condition.

The disciples of Jesus tried to cast the demon out of the boy, but failed. Luke recorded that as the boy went to Jesus, the demon caused him to react. Jesus commanded the spirit to leave and the child was delivered. Matthew recorded that Jesus rebuked the spirit, it departed, and the lad was cured that very hour.

Mark's record of this demonic encounter is more extensive than those of Matthew and Luke. He recorded that Jesus questioned the father as to how long the boy had been possessed. The father replied that the condition had existed from early childhood.

Jesus stressed to the father the importance of belief, then spoke to the deaf and mute spirit and told it to come out and enter no more. The spirit cried and came out leaving the boy in such a condition that many thought he was dead. But Jesus took him by the hand and lifted him up.

When the disciples asked Jesus why they were unable to cast out the demon, Jesus answered: "If you have faith as a mustard seed, you will say to this mountain, 'Move from here to there' and it will move; and nothing will be impossible for you. However, this kind does not go out except by prayer and fasting" (Matt. 17:20-21). His answer reveals the importance of faith, prayer, and fasting in dealing with demon spirits. It also proves that some demons are more difficult to cast out than others.

Incident: Demon possessed man in the synagogue (Mark 1:21-28; Luke 4:31-37)

Summary: Although this man was present in the synagogue, Jesus did not refer to him as a son of Abraham or indicate He was a follower of God.

Those present in a church fellowship may be unbelievers and demon possessed. Church attendance does not guarantee a born again experience or freedom from demon powers.

This possession included more than a single demon as evidenced by the spokesman referring to all of them as "us." When one of the demons began to speak, Jesus told it to "hold its peace." He rebuked all of the demons, and they tore the man, cried out, threw him down, and came out.

Those who witnessed this event marveled at the authority and power with which Jesus dealt with unclean spirits.

Incident: The blind and mute demoniac (Matt. 12:22-32; Mark 3:22-30; Luke 11:14-23)

Summary: Jesus healed this man, who could speak and see after the deliverance, by casting the demon out of him.

Jesus gave His most extensive teaching regarding casting out demons in connection with this deliverance. A summary of this teaching reveals:

- A house with division cannot stand. Demons call the bodies in which they reside their "house." Demons and the spirit of God cannot exist in the same house.
- Kingdoms or cities divided cannot stand.
- Satan cannot cast out Satan.

- Casting out demons is part of the ministry of God's kingdom.
- Demons are cast out by the Spirit of God.
- It is necessary to bind the strong man (the chief demon) before attempting to cast him out (spoil his works).
- There is no neutral ground in this spiritual battle. If you are not with Jesus, you are against Him.
- When an unclean spirit is cast out of a person, it seeks reentry into a human body.
- If the person from whom the demon has departed does not fill his spiritual house, the demon will return with other demons. The final condition of that person will be worse than in the beginning.

Incident: Demoniac of Gadarene (Matt. 8:28-34; Mark 5:1-20; Luke 8:26-39)

Summary: According to Matthew, two men possessed by demons, so fierce that no man could control them, lived in the tombs. Mark and Luke stressed the terrible condition and the deliverance of one of the two, whose condition was perhaps the worst ever encountered during the ministry of Jesus.

Many demons possessed these men. Both were so affected that they could not live in normal society.

The demons in one man called themselves "Legion" for they were many. They made it impossible to bind the man even with chains. The demons tormented him so badly that he wandered, cried out, cut himself with stones, and wore no clothing. But his demons recognized Jesus and asked if He had come to torment them before their time. "Their time" refers to their final judgment when they will be confined to the lake of fire (hell).

When He cast them out, Jesus permitted them to enter a herd of pigs, which resulted in the death of the pigs.

The residents of the city then asked Jesus to leave perhaps because pigs, which were their livelihood, were more important to them than the deliverance of men from demonic powers.

Other incidents: In addition to these specific encounters with demons, the Bible makes general references to Jesus' ministry to those affected by demons.

In Matthew 4:24 and Luke 6:18, the term *healed* describes how Jesus dealt with the demons.

In Mark 1:32-34, 39; 6:13, the term *cast out* describes His strategy.

Luke 4:41 simply records that the devils "came out." Luke 7:21 states that He "cured" them. Matthew 8:16 records that He "cast out the spirits with a word." And Mark 16:9 and Luke 8:2 state that Jesus cast seven devils out of Mary Magdalene.

Part Six: The Final Briefing

THE LAST GREAT BATTLE OF SPIRITUAL WARFARE

A great and final conflict will bring this spiritual war of the ages to a triumphant conclusion. Jesus will defeat Satan and his evil forces and will reign forever as King of kings.

In this concluding session of *Strategic Spiritual Warfare,* you will prepare for the final conflict.

15 PREPARE FOR THE FINAL CONFLICT

Objectives: Through this strategy session, you will learn to:

- Identify events preceding the final conflict
- Summarize events of the final conflict
- Explain Satan's final destiny
- Identify the time of judgment
- Achieve victory in the spirit world
- Apply the strategy of maintaining

Key Verses for This Study:

> The devil, who deceived them, was cast into the lake of fire and brimstone where the beast and the false prophet are. And they will be tormented day and night forever and ever. (Rev. 20:10)

> I also will keep you from the hour of trial which shall come upon the whole world. (Rev. 3:10)

> He laid hold of the dragon, that serpent of old, who is the Devil and Satan, and bound him for a thousand years; and he cast him into the bottomless pit, and shut him up, and set a seal on him, so that he should deceive the nations no more till the thousand years were finished. But after these things he must be released for a little while. (Rev. 20:2-3)

Step Fifteen: Prepare for the Final Conflict

> We must never view ourselves as experts in this matter of spiritual warfare. The moment we do, we become the victims of our enemy. Only total humble reliance upon the Lord Jesus Christ can secure our victory. Never let this subject of warfare with Satan and his kingdom divide you from your union with the body of believers.
>
> —*Mark I. Bubeck*

Final judgment upon Satan has already been pronounced through the death and resurrection of Jesus Christ. But this judgment will not be carried out until Jesus returns to earth.

This chapter concerns the final conflict, that last great spiritual battle in which all the forces of evil will fall in defeat. The final conflict will result in the crowning of our King, the establishment of the kingdom of God in visible form, and judgment of the spiritual forces of evil. It will be the final victory in spiritual warfare.

Events Preceding the Final Conflict

The Return of Jesus

The Bible teaches that the Lord will return to earth for believers. Jesus promised His followers, "I go to prepare a place for you. And if I go and prepare a place for you, I will come again and receive you to Myself; that where I am, there you may be also" (John 14:2–3).

Believers also refer to this return of Jesus as the rapture. First Thessalonians 4 provides details about the return of Jesus for believers.

- Jesus Himself will return (v. 16).
- Believers will be resurrected from the grave (v. 16).
- A "rapture" will occur: living believers will be taken from earth to meet Christ (v. 17).
- Believers who have died, believers living at the time of Christ's return, and the Lord Jesus Christ will be reunited (v. 17).

Some believe the rapture will occur before the tribulation (mentioned below) and that believers will not have to experience any of this terrible time on earth. Others believe the rapture will happen midway through this period. Still others believe the rapture will happen at the end of the tribulation. More important is to be prepared to go with Jesus no matter when or how He returns for His people. No one can know the exact time of this great event: "But of that day and hour no one knows, not even the angels of heaven, but My Father only" (Matt. 24:36).

Although we don't know the exact timing of the rapture, Jesus did identify some prophetic signs that will indicate when the time is near. Read about these in Matthew 24. List the events that will occur before the return of the Lord Jesus Christ.

_____
_____
_____

The Tribulation

The Bible tells of a terrible time on earth called the tribulation, during which the spiritual forces of evil will be more active than ever in the history of the world. Demons will do signs, wonders, and deceive many (Rev. 16:13–14). They will seek worship and condemn people with a special mark of ownership. Three things will distinguish the tribulation from all other times of trouble.

- *It will be worldwide, not just local.* "I also will keep you from the hour of trial which shall come upon the whole world" (Rev. 3:10).
- *People will realize the end of the world is near.* "And said to the mountains and rocks, 'Fall on us and hide us from the face of Him who sits on the throne and from the wrath of the Lamb! 'For the great day of His wrath has come, and who is able to stand?'" (Rev. 6:16–17).
- *The intensity of the trouble will be greater than ever before experienced.*

These intense judgments from God that will affect the earth are described in Revelation 6, 8, 9, and 16 and in Matthew 24:4–14. The world must be punished for sin and for rejecting God.

Summarize the conditions on earth during the tribulation.

_____
_____

What three things will distinguish the tribulation from other times of trouble?

_____
_____
_____

The Millennium

The millennium is a period of one thousand years after the tribulation, during which Jesus will rule the earth in righteousness. "And the LORD shall be King over all the earth. / In that day it shall be— / 'The LORD is one,' / And His name one" (Zech. 14:9). And the city of Jerusalem will be the center of government. "Now it shall come to pass in the latter days / That the mountain of the LORD's house / Shall be established on the top of the mountains, / And shall be exalted above the hills; / And all nations shall flow to it. . . . / For out of Zion shall go forth the law, / And the word of the LORD from Jerusalem" (Isa. 2:2-3).

Before the start of and during this millennial period, Satan and his evil forces will be bound. A great war will occur on earth. "[God] laid hold of the dragon, that serpent of old, who is the Devil and Satan, and bound him for a thousand years; and he cast him into the bottomless pit, and shut him up, and set a seal on him, so that he should deceive the nations no more till the thousand years were finished. But after these things he must be released for a little while" (Rev. 20:2-3).

Summarize the conditions on earth during the millennial period (also see Isa. 11:6-9):

_____

_____

The Final Conflict

After the thousand years, the final conflict with Satan will occur. "Now when the thousand years have expired, Satan will be released from his prison and will go out to deceive the nations which are in the four corners of the earth . . . to gather them together to battle, whose number is as the sand of the sea. They went up on the breadth of the earth and surrounded the camp of the saints and the beloved city [Jerusalem]" (Rev. 20:7-9). God will send fire from Heaven and end all opposition of the forces of evil.

This final battle will occur because Satan must be defeated and Jesus acknowledged as Lord of all. This will complete God's plan of the ages. This is the final battle in the spiritual warfare that has raged from the rebellion of Satan through the history of the world.

What is the reason for the final battle?

Summarize events occurring during the final battle.

Satan's Final Destiny

The devil, who deceived them, was cast into the lake of fire and brimstone where the beast and the false prophet are. And they will be tormented day and night forever and ever. (Rev. 20:10)

Then He will also say to those on the left hand, "Depart from Me, you cursed, into the everlasting fire prepared for the devil and his angels." (Matt. 25:41)

Demons themselves recognize their own destiny. When Jesus met the two demon-possessed men, the demons cried out to Him, "What have we to do with You, Jesus, You Son of God? Have You come here to torment us before the time?" (Matt. 8:29).

Describe the destiny of Satan and his demons.

The Time of Judgment

All unbelievers will be resurrected to face judgment. Because they did not repent from sin and accept Jesus as Savior they will be condemned to eternity in Hell:

> And I saw the dead, small and great, standing before God, and books were opened. And another book was opened, which is the Book of Life. And the dead were judged according to their works, by the things which were written in the books. The sea gave up the dead who were in it, and Death and Hades delivered up the dead who were in them. And they were judged, each one according to his works. Then Death and Hades were cast into the lake of fire. This is the second death. And anyone not found written in the Book of Life was cast into the lake of fire. (Rev. 20:12-15)

True believers who repented from sin and accepted Jesus as Savior will escape this terrible fate, and for them, the great spiritual battle will be over! "Then to Him was given dominion and glory and a kingdom, / That all peoples, nations, and languages should serve Him. / His dominion is an everlasting dominion, / Which shall not pass away. / And His kingdom the one / Which shall not be destroyed" (Dan. 7:14).

What is the destiny of unbelievers?

What is the destiny of believers?

Victory in the Spirit World

This chapter concludes this course on spiritual warfare. In reality, this side of Heaven you will never stop studying and learning about this subject. Just as a soldier in the natural world, you will continue to develop your skills and strategies as you battle the enemy.

We want to assure you that *you can be victorious over all the power of the enemy and in every battle of life.* Just remember:

- Your victory is assured, because it is not dependent upon *you* but upon God. "Who is this King of glory? / The LORD strong and mighty, / The LORD mighty in battle" (Ps. 24:8).
- God protects you in battle. "O GOD the Lord, the strength of my salvation, you have covered my head in the day of battle" (Ps. 140:7).
- If you become discouraged during battle, God will comfort you. "For indeed, when we came to Macedonia, our bodies had no rest, but we were troubled on every side. Outside were conflicts, inside were fears. Nevertheless God, who comforts the downcast, comforted us" (2 Cor. 7:5–6).
- God will encourage you in the midst of your warfare. "Do not fear, nor be afraid; / Have I not told you from that time, and declared it?" (Isa. 44:8 KJV).

> For I, the LORD your God, will hold your right hand,
> Saying to you, "Fear not, I will help you." (Isa. 41:13)

> I, even I, am He who comforts you.
> Who are you that you should be afraid
> Of a man who will die,
> And of the son of a man who will be made like grass?
>   (Isa. 51:12)

- No weapon formed against you will succeed. "No weapon formed against you shall prosper" (Isa. 54:17).
- You will attain victory over the world. "For whatever is born of God overcomes the world. And this is the victory that has overcome the world—our faith. Who is he who overcomes the world, but he who believes that Jesus is the Son of God?" (1 John 5:4–5).

- You will attain victory over the flesh. "And those who are Christ's have crucified the flesh with its passions and desires" (Gal. 5:24).
- You will attain victory over the devil. "And the God of peace will crush Satan under your feet shortly" (Rom. 16:20).
- You will attain victory over death and the grave. "I will ransom them from the power of the grave; / I will redeem them from death" (Hosea 13:14).
- You will attain victory over *all* that exalts itself against God. "Casting down arguments and every high thing that exalts itself against the knowledge of God" (2 Cor. 10:5).
- You will attain victory over *all* the power of the enemy. "Behold, I give you the authority . . . over all the power of the enemy" (Luke 10:19).
- And when the battle is over, you will stand victorious. "So use every piece of God's armor to resist the enemy whenever he attacks, and *when it is all over, you will still be standing up*" (Eph. 6:13 TLB).

You are now prepared to be an overcomer! God has made some beautiful promises to the overcomers. Claim these now by making a verbal confession of faith.

I am an overcomer and I will . . .

Eat of the tree of life: Revelation 2:7
Eat of hidden manna: Revelation 2:17
Be clothed in white raiment: Revelation 3:5
Be a pillar in the temple of God: Revelation 3:12
Sit with Jesus in His throne: Revelation 3:21
Have a new name: Revelation 2:17
Have power over the nations: Revelation 2:26
Have the name of God written upon me: Revelation 3:12
Have an intimate relationship with God: Revelation 21:7

Have the morning star (Jesus): Revelation 2:28
Be confessed by Jesus before God the Father: Revelation 3:5
Not be hurt by the second death: Revelation 2:11
Not have my name blotted out of the book of life: Revelation 3:5
Inherit all things: Revelation 21:7

The Strategy of Maintaining

If you have studied each chapter of *Strategic Spiritual Warfare* and completed all of the assignments, you have obtained a great deal of knowledge and experience that will enable you to wage spiritual warfare more effectively.

It is sometimes harder to *maintain* a thing than to *obtain* it. The Bible addresses this issue in a parable told by Jesus in Luke 19:12-26. As you read this passage, you will note that the servants who used and increased the money were given more money. The one who did nothing with the money he received lost it.

If you use what you have been given it will increase. "For I say to you, that to everyone who has will be given; and from him who does not have, even what he has will be taken away from him" (Luke 19:26).

To maintain what you have learned in this study, you must use it in your everyday life and ministry. You must apply the strategies of spiritual warfare and wage battle against the enemy. As you enter the battlefield, remember that the Captain of the Lord of Hosts marches beside you.

You will continue to fight spiritual battles until you go to be with the Lord. As you fight each battle, you will learn more about warfare from both your successes and your failures.

Always remember that failure is temporary. You may lose a battle now and then, but the final victory has been assured by our Lord of Hosts!

Bibliography

Barnhouse, Donald Grey. *The Invisible War.*
  Grand Rapids, MI: Zondervan, 1965.

Barrett, Ethel. *The Great Conflict.*
  Ventura, CA: Regal Books, 1969.

Basham, Don. *Deliver Us from Evil.*
  Washington Depot, CT: Chosen Books, 1972.

Billheimer, Paul. *Adventure in Adversity.*
  Wheaton, IL: Tyndale House Publishers, 1984.

_____. *Destined for the Throne.*
  Fort Washington, PA: Christian Literature Crusade, 1975.

_____. *The Technique of Spiritual Warfare.*
  Santa Ana, CA: Trinity Broadcasting Network.

Bounds, E. M. *Power Through Prayer.*
  Grand Rapids, MI: Baker Book House.

_____. *Satan, His Personality, Power, and Overthrow.*
  Grand Rapids, MI: Baker Book House, 1963.

Bubeck, Mark. *The Adversary.*
  Chicago, IL: The Moody Bible Institute, 1975.

Bussel, Harold L. *Unholy Devotion.*
  Grand Rapids, MI: Zondervan, 1983.

Chafer, Lewis Sperry. *Satan.*
  New York, NY: Gospel Publishing House, 1909.

Chambers, Oswald. *If You Will Ask.*
  Grand Rapids, MI: Discovery House Publishers, 1958.

  _____. *My Utmost for His Highest.*
  New York, NY: Dodd, Mead, and Company, 1935.

Demon Experiences in Many Lands.
  Chicago, IL: Moody Press, 1960.

Eareckson, Joni, and Steve Estes. *A Step Further.*
  Grand Rapids, MI: Zondervan, 1978.

Eastman, Dick. *A Celebration of Praise.*
  Grand Rapids, MI: Baker Book House, 1984.

  _____. *No Easy Road.*
  Grand Rapids, MI: Baker Book House, 1971.

Graham, Billy. *Angels: God's Secret Agents.*
  Garden City, NY: Doubleday and Company, 1975.

  _____. *Approaching Hoofbeats.*
  Waco, TX: Word Books, 1983.

Green, Michael. *I Believe in Satan's Downfall.*
  Grand Rapids, MI: W. B. Eerdmans Publishing Company, 1981.

Gurnall, William. *The Christian in Complete Armor.*
    Carlisle, PA: The Banner of Truth, 1989.

Harper, Michael. *Spiritual Warfare.*
    Plainfield, NJ: Logos International, 1970.

Hayford, Jack. *Prayer Is Invading the Impossible.*
    Plainfield, NJ: Logos International, 1977.

Herman, E. *Creative Prayer.*
    Cincinnati, OH: Forward Movement Publications.

Huegel, F. J. *Bone of His Bone.*
    Grand Rapids, MI: Zondervan, 1940.

LaHaye, Tim. *The Battle for the Mind.*
    Old Tappan, NJ: Fleming H. Revell Co., 1980.

Lewis, C. S. *The Screwtape Letters.*
    New York: Macmillan, 1961.

Lindsell, Harold. *The World, the Flesh, and the Devil.*
    Minneapolis, MN: World Wide Publications, 1973.

Lloyd-Jones, D. M. *Romans: The New Man.*
    Grand Rapids, MI: Zondervan, 1972.

MacNutt, Francis. *Healing.*
    Altamonte Springs, FL: Creation House, 1988.

Miller, C. Leslie. *All about Angels.*
    Ventura, CA: Regal Books, 1973.

BIBLIOGRAPHY

Murray, Andrew. *With Christ in the School of Prayer.*
    Springdale, PA: Whitaker House, 1981.

Nee, Watchman. *The Spiritual Man.*
    New York, NY: Christian Fellowship Publications, 1968.

Needham, David. *Birthright.*
    Portland, OR: Multnomah Press, 1979.

Needham, Mrs. George C. *Angels and Demons.*
    Chicago, IL: Moody Press.

Penn-Lewis, Jesse. *The Spiritual Warfare.*
    Dorset, England: The Overcomers Trust.

    _____. *War on the Saints.*
    Fort Washington, PA: Christian Literature Crusade.

Phillips, Coleman. *Your Spiritual Arsenal.*
    Old Tappan, NJ: Chosen Books, 1988.

Sanders, J. Oswald. *Satan Is No Myth.*
    Chicago, IL: Moody Press, 1975.

Swindoll, Charles R. *Dropping Your Guard.*
    Waco, TX: Word Books, 1983.

    _____. *Demonism.*
    Portland, OR: Multnomah, 1981.

Tozer, A. W. *The Pursuit of God.*
    Harrisburg, PA: Christian Publications, 1982.

Watson, David. *How to Win the War.*
    Wheaton, IL: Harold Shaw Publishers, 1972.

BIBLIOGRAPHY

———. *The Hidden Battle: Strategies for Spiritual Victory.*
    Wheaton, IL: Harold Shaw Publishers, 1980.

Wiersbe, Warren W. *The Strategy of Satan.*
    Wheaton, IL: Tyndale House Publishers, 1979.

Wimber, John. *Power Healing.*
    San Francisco, CA: Harper & Row, 1987.

Notes: Strategic Spiritual Warfare

Chapter 1

1. A question sometimes asked in regards to a person being born in sin is, "Do babies who die before they accept or reject Christ go to hell?" Although the Bible makes no mention of the doctrine of "the age of accountability," this silence does not disprove it. This doctrine teaches that our sins are not charged to us until we reach an age at which we can be accountable for our actions. It is our belief that children who die before they reach this age are ushered into the wonderful presence of God.
2. *Destined for the Throne* by Paul Billheimer is an excellent explanation of what God is doing to give us "on-the-job training" to prepare us for eternity.

Chapter 3

1. The word *Satan* means "opponent," "adversary," "false accuser." It is pronounced similarly in both Greek and Hebrew. Scripture addresses a real person, not an idea or concept. Lucifer (Hebrew: *heylel*) appears to be his more formal name, although the word itself refers to the morning star. It means "brightness." The root word (Hebrew: *halal*) from which it comes means to be "clear" or to "shine." The word *devil* (Greek: *diabolos*) also means "to accuse." Specifically it means "Satan." There is only one devil (Satan), but many agents employed under him are called *demons* (Greek: *daimonia*).
2. Some believe that Satan was an archangel as is the angel Michael, although Scripture does not specifically support the idea.

3. There are many ideas as to what demons actually are. It seems that most people believe they are the spirits of fallen angels dispossessed of their bodies. Another interesting idea is that they are the departed spirits of offspring from the cohabitation of the sons of God (supposedly angels) and the daughters of men (mankind) (see Gen. 6:1–6). The apocryphal book of Enoch supports this idea. Certainly "sons of God" in the book of Job are a reference to angels (1:6; 2:1; 38:3–7).
4. Paul's description of demon powers puts them in what appears to be ranks. The question then becomes, "Which are the strongest and most authoritative?" We believe "principalities" to be the least and those performing "spiritual wickedness in high places" to be the strongest. Others believe the reverse of this. Whichever is correct, the important thing is to recognize that there is a war going on, and demons are a part of it.

Chapter 6

1. E. M. Bounds, *The Necessity of Prayer* (Grand Rapids, MI: Baker, 1992), 79.
2. Recommended books on prayer:

Creative Prayer, E. Herman
The Hour That Changed the World, Dick Eastman
The Life of Reverend David Brainerd, Jonathan Edwards
The Necessity of Prayer, E. M. Bounds
No Easy Road, Dick Eastman
Power from on High, Charles G. Finney
The Power of Prayer, Herbert Lockyer
Power Through Prayer, E. M. Bounds
Prayer Is Invading the Impossible, Jack Hayford
Prevailing Prayer, Charles G. Finney.
Quiet Talks on Following the Christ, S. D. Gordon
The School of Christ, T. Austin-Sparks
When You Pray, Harold Lindsell

NOTES

Chapter 7

1. Charles Swindoll, *Demonism* (Portland, OR: Multnomah, 1981), 5.
2. Paul Billheimer, *Destined for the Throne* (Fort Washington, PA: Christian Literature Crusade, 1975), 98–99.
3. Ibid.

Chapter 10

1. Additional information on this subject can be found in Chapter 4 under the heading "The Relationship of the Spirit to the Flesh."

Chapter 14

1. See *Demon Experiences in Foreign Lands*, published by Moody Press, for a compilation of strange occurrences on foreign mission fields.
2. It is not known whether these men were true believers. Christians that either run ahead of or lag behind the leading of the Holy Spirit make easy targets for the enemy.

About the Authors

Rev. Ray Beeson is a graduate of Central Washington State College and holds a B.A. in mathematics with a teaching credential as well as an M.A. in secondary school administration.

He has taught public school for more than eight years and has served with the International Prayer Corps and World Literature Crusade, where he taught Change the World Schools of Prayer. He has also been a youth pastor.

Currently he serves as president and director of Overcomers Ministries in Ventura, California, and travels extensively, teaching primarily on the subjects of prayer and spiritual warfare.

Ray has authored *The Real Battle* (Tyndale House Publishers), *That I May Know Him* (Fleming H. Revell Company), *The Hidden Price of Greatness*—co-written with Ranelda Mack Hunsicker (Tyndale House Publishers), *Spiritual Warfare and Your Children*—co-written with Kathi Mills (Thomas Nelson Publishers), and *Create in Me a Clean Heart* (Thomas Nelson Publishers).

Dr. Patricia Hulsey is a graduate of California State University at Long Beach. She holds a M.A. degree in Christian School Administration from Western Graduate School and a Ph.D. from Trinity Theological Seminary.

Patricia served as principal of Garden Grove Christian School in Garden Grove, California, and as director of the World Evangelism School of Ministry in San Diego, California.

She has worked with students from seventy-six nations and has traveled to more than forty countries. She presently serves as vice president of Harvestime International Network, preparing training materials for national Christian leaders in Third World nations.

Patricia has published with the Full Gospel Businessmen's *Voice, The Christian Reader,* and *Evangel* magazines and has received an award for writing from the Evangelical Press Association. Her book *Bitter Waters* is an account of suffering and sorrow on a personal level.

www.ingramcontent.com/pod-product-compliance
Lightning Source LLC
Chambersburg PA
CBHW080433110426
42743CB00016B/3151